DISTRESSED PROPERTY

PROPERTY

SECRETS

DISTRESSED PROPERTY

PROPERTY

SECRETS

HOW ANYONE CAN SUCCEED
WITH REAL ESTATE INVESTING

LOGAN FULLMER

PALMETTO
PUBLISHING
Charleston, SC
www.PalmettoPublishing.com

Paperback ISBN: 9798318804113

We help men and women change their lives with real estate-based businesses using basic skills, education and their determination. Are you interested in getting started in the real estate investing industry or growing an existing career? Please visit www.loganfullmer.com, call 1-800-333-8108, or email info@greatvoice.com.

CONTENTS

CHAPTER ONE

WHEN THE PIPELINE RAN DRY

The sun was bright. The wind was hot. The fire-retardant clothing and steel-toe boots just made it hotter. The sun even warmed my hard hat.

I'd been out there for about four months this time. Deep South Texas. The ranch I was working on adjoined the Mexico border, and I could see the Rio Grande at times. I was at the tail end of a 12-inch pipeline construction project, recently promoted to project manager—from assistant, from project coordinator, from field clerk—all in about two years.

We were lowering 12-inch diameter pipe into a five-foot-deep, 24-inch-wide ditch and getting ready to backfill it, a mile at a time. Right through ranch cattle pens, under fences, even boring the pipeline under the occasional 150-year-old oak tree or a caliche ranch road. This was the Briscoe Ranch—one of the wealthiest and most prolific oil ranches in Texas. The place was littered with pipelines below the surface, but above it, all you could see was dust, a little grass, a bunch of mesquite trees, well-kept low fences, and trophy whitetail deer running all over the place—usually at dawn and again at dusk.

My crew got a chance to work straight through, so we'd been out there over four weeks without a day off. We were into overtime by Wednesday every week, so the money was damn good—the best money I'd made in my life at that time. I stood there looking across a field that looked just like the last mile, and the mile before that, and the mile before that. Everything looked the same down there—just a different pipe joint, just a different day, and of course a different time clock card.

It was the worst place a man could be in Texas—but it was the best place I'd ever been in my life, at the time. I stood straight and tall, no matter how tired I was. I had a good group of guys working. I had a group of people back in the office in George West, Texas, who trusted me. I was working like a dog, but I was happier than a pig in shit.

By this point, I'd been with the construction company in the oil field for a couple of years. I showed up fresh out of a detox center in Austin, Texas, just trying to make right what I hadn't gotten right in the first 25 years of my life. Those years were tough. Growing up I wasn't abused or anything, but my parents' separation really got to me. When poverty set in, I kind of felt worthless. Dad wasn't not great at earning a living while he drank from dusk til dawn for his entire adult life. My friends' parents were tradesmen or lawyers. We were pretty damn poor—living in a house that was seller-financed to my dad with a down payment from my grandma that was obviously never paid back. Few window units and its most recent model had been forty years before we moved in.

One day I got a call from a college friend, Shawn Shipman, we were catching up, I needed work, and he could sense it. He asked if I wanted to come work with him in the oilfield. That day he'd saved my life, and didn't event know it. He got me a job, I packed my bags and was in Deep South Texas in two days for the interview and was hired on the spot. First time I could pass a drug test in ten years. I was looking for something to change. I sure found what I was looking for.

Something changed when I got way out there in the oil field. I was so far away from heroin and pills—and alcohol, for that matter—I couldn't find them if I wanted to. By this point, the oil field had cleaned up pretty good. And so had I.

I was just looking for one more chance to make things right. And this time, it worked.

I'd put together more sober days than I ever had in my life. I'd also built some real self-esteem out there, and I'd piled quite a bit of cash in my bank account. I wasn't going to blow it this time. I meant the sobriety—and the money.

Several years back, I inherited a huge sum of money from my grandparents. Within about three years, I blew every penny. Two generations of savings, their whole net worth, two farms- all up in smoke. Or in my arm, you could say. This time, money was different. I knew I'd burned a lifetime's worth of inheritance in just a few years. Now I was earning like a normal man, and it didn't come in as fast. I realized it would take me fifteen to twenty years—maybe more—to earn what I'd blown in just three or four.

So this time, I saved every penny. I was judicious with every dime—almost to the point of being a miser. I wasn't going to waste it all. Not this time. This was different. They say no man crosses the same stream twice, for he's not the same man, and it's not the same water. This was not the same man, nor the same money. This money was better. It was mine. Actually mine. I earned this money, every dollar, with my bare hands.

But in that exact moment, all was good. I had a couple hundred grand in the bank. I finally had self-confidence again. Most importantly, I was sober and clean. Things were clicking. I finally got to the point where I felt like a man. I could pay my own bills. I didn't ask anybody for anything. And I started to get a little self-respect. That's all I ever wanted in life. And I finally found it—out here, in the nastiest field in the middle of one of the biggest oil fields in the United States. In that moment, it hit me like a ton of bricks: I couldn't have been more satisfied. But as quickly as that feeling of happiness and satisfaction came, it immediately left. I didn't feel right. I almost felt cheated. Just as I understood that I'd made it to this level, I knew there was more. I was so happy to be here, yet I knew I had so far to go.

Something changed that day. Before this, I'd just set my sights on minimum hurdles—just trying to get out of the hole, just trying to be as good as the average guy around town. But in that moment, it vanished. That wasn't good enough anymore. I knew there was more, and I had to go figure it out.

As quickly as the smile left my face, a couple of tears ran down my cheeks—the same as they did while writing this paragraph.

I got in my truck, looked in the rearview mirror at my own reflection, and knew something had to change. There was more for me out there, and it was about time I found it.

That night, I stayed up almost all night in the little 14-foot RV I'd bought for cash so I could save my per diem. I was being paid $95 a day in per diem—about $1,500 a month—and lot rent was only $500. That added another thousand bucks to the war chest each month. I stayed up late Googling, staring at the wall, thinking. Dreaming with my eyes open. Things were running through my mind so fast I couldn't collect all my thoughts. But looking back, it was just a process that had to happen. It got me off dead center. A couple of days later, I took the weekend off. All the crews went home to see their families. But me—being single—just went to San Antonio for the weekend and rented a hotel. I caught up with old friends from college, drove around the city looking at old, crummy houses and vacant lots. The feeling of change was coursing through my veins. Maybe even a little anxiety. I was behind again, well in my mind I was. That made it real. I felt like my future was out there in that town—but I just couldn't quite see it yet.

I talked to a couple of buddies who were in real estate. They were enthralled with big projects and building a name for themselves. I just wanted to earn more money. I didn't care about having my name on a building.

Eventually, I started poking through the tax records and deed records. That's when I realized how much vacant land there was on the east side of San Antonio. Many of these lots were assessed by the tax office at only $5,000. That stunned me. San Antonio is the seventh-largest city in the United States, and these were 5,000-square-foot lots—big enough to build on—with utilities, curbs, gutters, and electric poles.

You could literally buy a buildable lot in the seventh-largest city in America for about $5,000.

Remember, I'd spent a lifetime's worth of savings in just a few years, so at this point I was far more concerned about loss than upside. Of course I wanted upside, but I couldn't stomach losing again. I figured: worst case, I buy a bunch of lots, and if the plan fails, someone will probably buy them from me for close to what I paid. If I lose, maybe I sell them for $4,000 apiece instead of $5,000. I didn't have $5,000 at risk—I only had $1,000.

I felt good about that downside. But I also remembered what happened in parts of Houston, East Austin, and Dallas—how worthless land turned into multi-million-dollar parcels when the bull economy ran upwards in the mid 2000s. I figured those were odds I was willing to bet on.

By the end of the weekend, I'd made up my mind.

As I packed my bags and headed back down to South Texas to finish the pipeline project, every mile I drove south made me want to turn around. Go back to San Antonio and get started. But I couldn't. I wasn't ready. I needed to earn more money, because I didn't think my time had come just yet. The desire was burning—but that's about all I had.

For the next year, I kept coming back to San Antonio and buying land. I would go into the tax records—this was way before deal-finding software—and manually make notes, creating lists of delinquent property. I'd find the owner's address, knock on doors, and show up with a Texas Real Estate Commission contract and $100 option money in cash. I didn't even know how to fill out the contract—I had to call my mom for help.

Didn't know how to pitch, no script. I just said what made sense.... "looks like you gave up on this property, mind if I take it off your hands and maybe take a run at it myself." No training, just desire and hunger. Nothing on the line except self respect. That was plenty. I couldn't face myself if I failed. There were no options, just kept trying because giving up was not an option.

So I tried different pitches til I found one that worked. And work, it did.

I started putting together as many deals as I could. One after the other. No real plan on what to do with them yet, just hoping they would increase in value or I could build spec homes for sale on them. I don't know. I just did it. Took about two years to build up that little portfolio.

Then. Out out of the blue. I was walking into a meeting at work. By this time I'm working in the main headquarters in San Antonio. Bidding work and managing projects controls. Then, it happened, I got the call. One of the most pivotal causes of my entire life.

A realtor called me. His name was Scott Malouff, and he and his understudy Jev, offered $200,000 for a property I had about $20,000 into. I'd had my head down, buying property, not paying much attention to the market. Turns out, it had moved. Speculators and builders had taken the east side by surprise, all around me and I hadn't noticed.

At that point, I might've had a couple dozen lots—maybe $300,000 into them. And here I was, selling one for nearly $200,000. I'd mostly capitalized.

That was a wild summer. The price of oil dropped, capital projects dried up, and I got laid off. But that same summer, I sold my first vacant lot, made $200,000, and I had a decision to make. Was I a real estate man, or was I an oilfield hand?

I took three days off. I ate well, slept better, and exercised like hell. The endorphins did me good. By the end of that week, it was clear—I was a real estate man.

And I never looked back.

My name is Logan Fullmer and this is the story of how I got rich flipping distressed property.

CHAPTER TWO

MAKE MONEY WITH DISTRESSED PROPERTY, NO B.S.

Every day, thousands of men and women just like you are making great money in the distressed property business with their mobile phone, internet access, inexpensive online based data, an Internet connection, and a little training.

They're called distressed property flippers, and they're flipping everything from single family homes, vacant lots, mobile homes, even commercial properties like warehouses and small apartments sometimes, for remarkable profits. This type of flipping is the absolute most capital efficient model in the business, since property can be purchased for as little as five hundred dollars. That is not a mistype or fluke, it is where the offers to sellers generally start and many times conclude. Its on the lower end of the spend, but its not uncommon.

Each year, tens of thousands of investors buy properties on the multiple listing services that need cosmetic remodels, land that needs to be cleaned up and soon to be cash flowing commercial property, unknowingly from distressed property flippers who usually earn multiples of what the investors do. The front end paperwork and title clearing experts are the best paid in the investment grade real estate food chain. Period.

The money-making opportunities for today's title clearing and ownership dispute resolving flippers go way beyond the small flip house in your neighborhood. I've identified countless markets, some of which are enjoying explosive growth, and I'll explain what those look like in this book.

Some people think that the big investors get all the best deal- but actually, that's not true. Sure, big timers get deals, but their business is normally less adaptive and moves far too slow to handle the deals that earn the huge margins. These deals are so unsuspecting and there's probably one in your neighborhood, no matter if you live in hundred thousand dollar homes, or one million dollar homes, its happened there.

However, large cities have tens of thousands of properties that have been abandoned, are delinquent on property tax payments, and or have title and ownership disputes. Additionally, as many as 500 homes are posted for foreclosure per month in large cities, totaling approximately 30,000 to 40,000 monthly foreclosures across the United States. A small handful of large investment firms can't do all of that work. There are plenty to go around. Heck, my companies transact hundreds annually, and we have not scratched the surface.

Most of the men and women who make money in the real estate investing space are people just like you. They work from their homes or coffee shops across the country earning six figures, many seven figures annually — and, by the way, don't think you have to spend a fortune on data, platforms, programs and systems. You can set up a basic lead generating pipeline for only a few hundred dollars — more about that coming up. I honestly began my business with a laptop, yellow pad and a monthly paycheck from my 9-5 job.

For some of these men and women, real estate is a full-time career. For others, it's an enjoyable way to make some extra money on the side: a money-making hobby, if you will. My program manger in my business office, who manages administrative work, just closed a hundred thousand dollar profit flip, in her spare time. And all she did was buy it two days before the foreclosure and put twenty grand in the property owners pocket. That owner was prepared to let the home foreclose and be gone forever. Instead the owner let Shelly buy it for a great price. Shelly has no formal training, just heard the chatter I the office and watched a few training videos and got after it.

The great news is, with the explosive growth of flipping shows on cable tv, YouTube education, and social medias coverage of home investors, there's an enormous, increasing need for investment grade property with clear title for flippers to renovate, subdivide or build on. That is our job, to supply that product.

You probably have lots of questions about how to get started in distressed property investing, as well as some questions about whether you have what it takes.

Well, I'm happy to help because the keys to distressed property investing success are probably not what you think. To be successful in the industry, you don't need huge experience, you don't need to invest a lot of money, and you don't need big time business connections.

All it takes is understanding a few key secrets and a great mentor who will train and guide you to help you follow the right road map to success.

CHAPTER THREE

WHY I WROTE THIS BOOK

As you know, my name is Logan Fullmer. Whether or not you recognize my name, you would recognize my business if you knew what to look for. I'm the guy who has quietly acquired that vacant home in your neighborhood, office building by your kids school, or the warehouse near your job, and sold it for outsized profit to an investor who is the person you saw show up with the crews and fix it up. My work, and other who do my same work, are all across the country, quietly cleaning up neighborhoods, and getting rich as the same time. I've been at this since about 2014, and have made tens of millions of dollars annually with my basic tools, and have trained hundreds, maybe even thousands of investors to do the same the course of a long and successful career.

I've never been featured in the New York Times or any other big publications, never been on national TV, but I have built a business with twenty incredibly people who help me transact hundreds of interests in properties each year, and earn tens of millions of dollars doing it. My wife and I have four children, live in a 100-year-old estate in the most prestigious neighborhood in San Antonio, Texas, we vacation in places like the Hamptons and generally travel private for work. Life is good at this point.

But it wasn't always that way. You read already who I used to be. When I had the day job, working the oilfield — but it wasn't just any day job. It was hard work.

It was not glamourous, it was long hours, weeks in a row, and zero flexibility, but that is what it took to get me one step closer to real estate. How you ask, well that is what this book is all about. And you know what? I truly am glad to help. I am passionate about entrepreneurship and believe that America's small businesses are the backbone of our great nation. I'm proud that I've helped create jobs, businesses, and that my once small business provides lasting value for many households, and of course, I'm proud of the wonderful life that I've created for myself.

But most importantly, it makes me happy to help you because sharing these secrets with others has changed lives, gotten folks out of the rat race, and frankly, I have a long list of people who have called me afterwards and told me that I am the reason they are because a millionaire. That is the most gratifying thing at this point in my career. And now, I want to pay it forward. Here's how it works.

CHAPTER FOUR

THE GAME THAT CHANGED MY LIFE

You're holding something different in your hands. This isn't some recycled real estate fluff or "guru" nonsense regurgitated for likes and followers. What you're about to read is exactly how I built a multi-million-dollar business from distressed, forgotten, problem-riddled properties that nobody else wanted to touch. Frankly, no one knew how to fix, it until I showed up.

This book is not a theory. It's not a sales pitch. It's not some abstract funnel dream. It's ten years of blood, sweat, deals, mistakes, and checks—broken down into a repeatable model I've built and scaled repeatedly.

And the truth is, it didn't start pretty. I was broke. I had a rough history with money, substance, and bad decisions. I had no connections, investor network, or secret mentor pulling strings. What I had was a decision: I wasn't going to keep living small. I wasn't going to keep trading hours for dollars. I wasn't going to keep screwing up.

So I picked up the phone, started calling, and started solving the kinds of problems that everyone else runs from. And that—right there—is where the money lives.

This book is for the hungry. The ones willing to take responsibility. The ones ready to work smarter than the rest. The ones who don't need it to be easy—just need it to be real.
If that's you, then let's get after it.

Here's the #1 secret to success in distressed property investing he shared.

I was once told the most important key to winning in this business is finding the right mentor.

A mentor is crucial — because in distressed real estate, especially when dealing with title issues, legal gray areas, and fractured ownership, you can't always see the full picture from the inside. You're too close to the deal. Too emotionally or financially invested to spot the cracks.

Have you ever looked back at a deal and thought, "How did I miss that?" Or maybe you passed on something that turned out to be a gold mine for someone else? That's what I'm talking about. To succeed in this niche, you need an outside set of eyes. Someone who's walked through dozens — maybe hundreds — of these kinds of deals and knows where the hidden traps (and hidden value) are. And just as important, you need a mentor who can show you how to build a real business out of solving these complex problems. And unless you want to pave the way like I did and take ten years to learn in all on you own… you need help.

Now don't get me wrong — I'm not stepping away from this game. Not even close. I am a shareholder in many businesses that do this work. I collect distributions for my investments in people and businesses over time, and that time of build with my head down has created time for me today. Time for me to work on passion projects. But I am entering a new chapter. I'm expanding the operation and launching new projects. That means I'll only have time to work with a small number of serious newcomers — people who actually appreciate the power of what I've learned and are ready to use it. I do have time, but its still got limitations. I was sort of passed the torch from some of the attorneys who helped me piece this together, when I was just figuring it out. And now, I want to pass it to you — but only if you're someone who sees the opportunity and is ready to act on it.

If you're not serious about building something real, that's fine — but this isn't for you. If you are honest, action-driven, and committed to doing the work... then keep reading. Because nothing fires me up more than helping someone go from "interested" to "in the game — and getting paid."

How to Know If Distressed Property Flipping Is for You

Could you see yourself in your comfortable home office, not adhering to a dress code, and working on interesting, creative projects that feel more like play than work — projects that you'll be proud of?

Would you enjoy an opportunity where no one is breathing down your neck — where you get to work when and where you choose? Do you know or suspect that you've been given the gift of a deal making, and do you want the recognition and satisfaction of sharing that gift with property sellers and investors? Maybe you did some negotiating at one point in your life or in your early days, and those were very exciting times in your life.

Are you looking for a way to supplement your income working from home, or even replace it, a money-making hobby, as I call it? You can't deny that, in today's economy, everyone needs additional streams of income — some sort of gig on the side. Some keep a side gig like Mike, who was a retired firefighter and successful real estate investor during his retirement. Some make it full time like Chris, who left his old line of work to flip distressed property full time, bringing in over a million dollars in his first year. Do you have a spouse, friend, or loved one in the real estate business that you've always admired, and are you exploring this opportunity as they exposed it to you? Do you imagine that this would be the perfect way to spend your career, or even your active retirement years? I've seen it both ways.

But whether your goal is part-time income or an exciting new career, you might be feeling frustrated by the lack of to-the-point real estate guidance. Or maybe you're looking for an experienced, caring mentor to take you by the hand and show you the way. That's why you're reading this book right now.

CHAPTER FIVE

WHERE IT ALL STARTED

"From Fence Posts to Foreclosures: My Path to Finding the Gold in the Problems Everyone Avoided"

Let me tell you something — people love to talk about their wins once they've already got the Rolex, the podcast, and the million-dollar portfolio. But nobody wants to tell you what it looked like at the beginning, when you're broke, hungover, in debt, and trying to pretend like everything's fine. I'll tell you, for me, it didn't start with some brilliant strategy or family mentor walking me through a textbook real estate deal. It started with me losing almost everything and realizing I didn't want to live like that anymore.

The path that led me to distressed property wasn't straight, and it sure as hell wasn't clean. It was messy, full of dumb mistakes, lost time, wasted money, and a few hard resets I'm not proud of. But I wouldn't change it — because that rocky road is exactly what made me sharp, made me hungry, and taught me how to see value where others saw trash.

This chapter is where it all kicks off. This is the real beginning — not the beginning with office leases and closings, but the one that involves cheap beer, hot summers, and hustling like your rent depends on it — because it did.

Back before I ever made a dime in real estate, I was just another broke dude trying to figure it out. I grew up in Temple, Texas — not exactly a hotbed for high finance. It was a small town with small-town values. My dad was a CPA, my mom was a real estate agent, and after they split, things weren't exactly cozy. There were tight months, lean Christmases, and a whole lot of watching my mom hustle to keep us afloat. Watching her sell houses with a phone in one hand and dinner in the other left a mark on me — and not the kind you see right away. But over time, it planted something in me: I didn't want to struggle. I didn't want to be just getting by.

Now, I'll be honest — I didn't jump out of high school into ambition. It took me seven years to finish college, and I spent most of those years drinking, partying, being a dumbass. I had consistent jobs but nothing sexy-installed car radios, did some sales for a homebuilder, and even started a fence-building business with a buddy from high school. That one almost went somewhere, too, until the oil field came calling.

It was my buddy Sean Shipman who lit the spark. He called me up one day and said, "Logan, are you tired of making no money?" At the time, I was just scraping by. He offered me a job in the oil patch making $100,000 a year. And to a guy who'd never cracked fifty, that sounded like the big time. I packed my bags and headed to South Texas.

The oil field was something else. I'd never worked harder. I'd never been more alone. But that solitude — man, that's where the fire started. I was living in a man camp, surrounded by a bunch of other guys chasing paychecks. I worked 70, sometimes 80 hours a week. And I didn't spend. I saved. I had nothing to blow money on, and I wasn't wasting my time in bars anymore. I was clean and sober, and for the first time in my life, I was scared to lose what I had. I was also happy. It was the happiest I'd been in life to date. I wasn't rich yet— but I had direction.

Now, here's the twist: before I even landed in the oil patch, I got a windfall. My grandmother passed away and left me an inheritance. We inherited land, stocks, and cash. My siblings and I split a seven-figure estate. At the time, I thought it was my golden ticket. But I wasn't ready. I pissed away most of it on cars, travel, and shot it up my arm — fast. Three years later, I had next to nothing to show for it. That money came and went so damn quick, it's embarrassing to say out loud. But it's the truth. And that pain — the shame of blowing what generations before me had built — became my fuel. I only had $5K left, a month's worth of expenses before I went to the oilfield.

So when I got to the oil field, I started clawing back. And not just money — confidence. Discipline. I learned to trust myself. I didn't buy cars or toys. I bought time. I stacked checks. And by year three, I'd stashed away a couple hundred grand, scared to lose it again. But I also knew — if I wanted out of the oil field, I had to make that money grow.

Here's where real estate re-entered the picture. I didn't have a roadmap, didn't have a mentor. But I knew this much: I didn't want to flip houses, borrow hard money, and pray I didn't get stuck with a leaky roof and a pissed-off contractor. I wanted something safer. That's when I found land.

I'd come home to San Antonio on weekends, and I noticed these little vacant lots in the downtown area — 5,000 square feet, paved street, utility access — selling for five, maybe ten grand. I was stunned. I'd always assumed downtown real estate was out of reach. But these were sitting there, doing nothing, and nobody seemed to want them.

So I started knocking on doors. I'd go to the Bexar County Appraisal District website, look up who owned a vacant lot, and then just drive to their house and knock. I didn't know anything about sourcing. This was 2013, 2014. Nobody was teaching this stuff on YouTube. I was just following my gut.

And guess what? People sold. I picked up lots for a few thousand bucks. Over time, I assembled a little portfolio of downtown dirt. Fast forward a few years — the oil market crashed and I got laid off. At the time, I'd sunk about $300,000 of my own money into 20-30 lots downtown. I figured I was going to sit on them for a decade.

Then I get a call. A realtor wants to buy one of my lots — and offers me $190,000. I bought that lot for $20,000. I thought it was a joke. But it closed. And suddenly, I wasn't broke anymore.

More importantly, I saw the model.

I didn't get rich flipping houses. I didn't get rich borrowing big checks from hard money lenders. I got rich solving the problems nobody else wanted to deal with — figuring out where the value was that others overlooked.

I was onto something. I just didn't know how big it could be. Not yet.

CHAPTER SIX

LEARNING TO SEE
WHAT OTHERS IGNORE

"Why Distressed Property Is Where the Real Money Hides"
After that first big win — that unexpected $190,000 offer on a lot I'd barely remembered buying — something shifted in me. It wasn't just the money. Yeah, the check was great. But what hit harder was the realization that I'd accidentally stumbled into something powerful. I had found value where no one else had looked. And it wasn't because I was smarter than anyone. It was because I'd taken a different path. I wasn't reading from the same playbook as every flipper and wholesaler out there. Hell, I didn't even own a playbook yet.

See, everyone else was looking for what was easy — clean houses, motivated sellers, something you could lock up in 10 minutes and wholesale for five grand. But these vacant lots? They were messy. They had multiple owners. They had liens. They were behind on taxes. The owners didn't even think the property was worth anything. Truth be told, at the time I bought them they weren't, but I got lucky the land appreciated quickly as the market was recovering from the 2008 mortgage crisis. I didn't know it yet, but this was the beginning of a whole business model — one built on solving problems, not just doing deals.

When I got laid off from the oil field, I didn't panic. I had already gotten a chunk of my investment back from that big sale, and I had a bunch of land left. I was still a little light on cash but heavy on equity. And I realized something most people never slow down long enough to see: the distress is where the discounts are. The problems are where the profit lives. I wasn't afraid of the mess anymore. I'd lived in chaos. I'd survived it. I could navigate it.

So I started building a strategy around that simple idea: find the messiest properties that no one else wants — the ones with delinquent taxes, multiple owners, code violations, busted titles — and learn how to clean them up. If I could do that, I could name my price. And my price started as little as $500 at times. Yes for real. But this wasn't a course or a YouTube tutorial. Nobody was teaching this. Not really. I had to learn by doing. And by screwing up. I remember one deal where I thought I had a clean title. The owner was ready to sign, the price was right, and everything looked good. Got it under contract, sent it to the title, and boom — title defect. Turns out there was a deed from 20 years ago that was never properly recorded. The title company said, "Sorry, we can't insure this." I was gutted. But instead of walking away, I got on the phone with an attorney and asked what it would take to fix it. He gave me a path. I followed it. Took six weeks, but I got it done. And I made $85,000 on that deal. That's when it clicked — these weren't roadblocks. These were filters. Barriers to entry. Most people saw a headache and walked. I saw a pay raise.

Do you want to know the secret to distressed property? It's not data. It's not skip tracing. It's not some fancy CRM. It's this: you have to be willing to go where other people won't. You have to be willing to make the second call when the first one doesn't answer. You have to be willing to track down Aunt Linda in another state to sign a release on an inherited property. You have to be willing to sit in the courthouse digging through probate liens and releases to find the missing document because no one else will.

Most of all — you have to be honest.

I learned early on that distressed sellers aren't stupid. They're scared. They're overwhelmed. They're stuck. But they're not dumb. And if you show up with slick talk and false promises, they can smell it a mile away. I learned to be honest — brutally honest — even when it cost me the deal. I'd tell people straight up, "Look, I might make a ton of money on this. If I can fix it and sell it, it's a big payday. But if I screw it up, I might lose money. Either way, I'm taking a risk. If you want to fix it yourself and go get top dollar, I'll tell you exactly how to do that. But if you want me to take it off your plate, I'm gonna need a good deal." Some of them sold to me and some did not. I don't need every deal in the world, there are plenty to go around.

And you know what? People respected that. That's why sellers started choosing me — not because I had the highest offer, but because I was real with them. I told them the truth. And in a world full of liars, that alone made me stand out.

It didn't take long before I started tracking patterns. I asked myself one big question: Where were my best deals coming from? And I don't mean best in terms of easiest — I mean the ones that made the most money.

So I went back and analyzed every deal I'd done in those early years. Every single one of the big wins — the $50K, $80K, $100K hits — they all had one thing in common: delinquent taxes.

Not fancy list stacking. Not probate mailing. Not driving for dollars. Just plain old unpaid taxes.

That was the smoke. And where there's smoke — you better believe there's fire.

So that became my main lead source. I went straight to the county tax offices, pulled the delinquent tax roll, and started calling. I didn't overthink it. I didn't build a perfect system. I just called the people who owed back taxes and asked if they wanted to sell. And buddy — the floodgates opened.

I'll break it down for you even simpler: Most people chase deals that look easy and clean. I chose the ones that look broken, ugly, and damn near impossible — because that's where the money is. The harder the problem, the bigger the spread.

And that's what this whole business model is built on.

In the next chapter, I'm going to walk you through exactly why distressed property isn't just a good investment — it's the smartest use of capital in today's market, especially in volatile times.

But before we go there, just remember this:

When everyone else is running away from the mess — run straight toward it. There's money in the mess.

CHAPTER SEVEN

THE MATH THAT MAKES IT ALL WORK

"Why Distressed Property Blows Up Your Profit Margins"

Now, let's get into the numbers — the part that most folks either get wrong or don't understand well enough to commit to this model. This chapter isn't just about spreadsheets and margins. It's about how you make decisions that build wealth — not just active income. It's where we separate the hustlers from the business owners, the weekend warriors from the folks building generational income.

Early on, when I was doing my first few distressed deals, I didn't have a ton of sophistication. I wasn't sitting behind five monitors, tracking every percentage point. Hell, I wasn't even using a CRM yet. But what I did have a few huge advantages: I understood risk. And I was willing to work hard. I was also willing to think things all the way through. Most folks, won't do that.

Remember, I'd already blown through a family inheritance. I knew what it felt like to have money — and then not have it. So when I got serious about investing again, I wasn't chasing the upside. I was protecting the downside. That mindset — that instinct to ask, "What happens if this goes wrong?" — is the only reason I survived those first few years. And it's why I still structure every deal the way I do today.

Let's break it down.

Let's say I find a property worth $100,000 as it sits. Not ARV — not "after repair value." We don't use that word in my office. That's a dirty word in my world. ARV means construction, contractors, permits, and timelines. I'm not in the renovation business. I'm in the velocity-of-money business.

So if the as-is value is $100K, I want to be buying that property somewhere between $30K and $60K — ideally closer to $30K. That means if I just clean it up, mow the lawn, remove the trash, and throw it on the MLS, I can sell it quickly for 90 to 95 cents on the dollar. Sometimes I even undercut the market and sell it at 85 cents to move it faster. Remember — speed is money. Additionally, giving a good deal, and giving a good deal is a theme that I live by, it also encourages me to price.

You might think, "Why not squeeze out the full value? Why leave money on the table?" Let me explain something most people don't get until they've sat on a property for six months: a fast nickel beats a slow dime. Every damn time. If I can turn that $30K into $90K in 30 days, I'll take it. Because I'm not just looking at one deal — I'm looking at an entire inventory. My cash has to keep moving. Now compare that to the traditional fix-and-flipper. They buy that same house at $70K, spend $30K fixing it up, spend six months dealing with city inspectors and flaky contractors, and sell it for

$150K. After interest, taxes, insurance, and realtor commissions, they clear — maybe — $25,000 to $30,000.

So what did they do? They risked twice as much capital, worked three times as long, and made less than I did reselling it without touching a hammer. And that's if everything goes right.

I'd rather make $40K three times in twelve months than make $30K once in six months. Period. That's the math that makes this whole model explode.

Here's another key point: distressed property is a capital-efficient model.

You don't need big loans. You don't need to go borrow $500K from hard money lenders and cross your fingers that the comps still make sense when the rehab's done. My average deal? We ran the numbers recently — our average purchase price was $48,000. Our average sale price was $194,000.

That's a $146,000 gross margin. After closing costs, realtor fees, and overhead, we net about $125,000. And remember — I didn't borrow a dime for that deal. That was straight cash.

That's not a fluke, either. That's what happens when you target the properties no one else wants. You get to name your price because there's no competition. You're solving a problem — not just bidding on a product.

Now let's talk about risk for a second, because that's where this model really shines.

2023-2024, when interest rates skyrocketed and the market slowed to a crawl, I watched seasoned flippers lose their shirts. These are the same guys that were bragging in 2020 about how they couldn't miss. They were buying 30 houses at a time and selling them before the paint was dry. Then the rates jumped. Buyers vanished. Inventory stacked up. Prices softened.

Suddenly, those guys were stuck. And because their margins were slim, to begin with, they had to come to the table with $30K, $50K per property just to close and pay off their lenders. Some of them declared bankruptcy. Others just walked away from deals and burned their reputations to the ground. Few, very few had enough to make good on the demands on their cash and save their reputation.

Me? I just lowered my price.

I was into each deal for 30, maybe 50 cents on the dollar. So even when I had to sell at 70 or 75 cents to move something fast, I still made money. I didn't have lenders breathing down my neck. I didn't have hard money payments piling up. I had control. And in a down market, control is everything. Cash is King. The golden rule…He who has the cash makes the rules.

The Cycle Time Advantage

Here's something else nobody talks about — cycle time. That's the time it takes from acquisition to exit. In the distressed property model, our average cycle time is 90 to 120 days. That means I can turn my capital over 3-4 times a year.

If I put $50,000 to work and double it in 120 days, that means I could — in theory — turn $50K into $100K, then $200K, $400K, and so on. Now, obviously, there are operational realities like overhead burdens and some mistakes here and there that prevent perfect reinvestment cycles, but the principle stands. Fast cash cycles multiply wealth faster than big one-time hits.

Flippers and buy-and-hold folks don't have that advantage. Their cash gets trapped in deals. That's why they constantly need new capital. They're on the debt treadmill. I'm not.

Big Margins = Big Flexibility

There's one last reason I chase distressed property above all else: big margins make your business bulletproof.

Life happens. Deals fall apart. Lawsuits pop up. Partners flake. If you're running a high-margin business, you can absorb those hits. If you're scraping by on 10% profits, one mistake can end your company.

But when you're making 2X, 3X, or even 5X on your investment — you can make mistakes, absorb surprises, and still end up with a win. That's how I sleep at night. That's why I'm not scared of downturns.

And the best part? This isn't just a business model. It's a **moat**.

Most people aren't willing to do what it takes to get these deals. They don't want to deal with 17 owners, call countless creditors, dig through dusty court files, or call the neighbor to track down a missing cousin. They'd rather chase the same overpriced PPC leads as everyone else and wonder why they can't win deals.

Good. Let them.

Because that leaves more opportunity for me — and for folks like you, if you're willing to go the extra mile.

CHAPTER EIGHT

HOW TO ACTUALLY FIND THESE DEALS

The Lead Source That Built My Business

You can't build a business if you don't have leads. And not just any leads. You need the right kind of leads—the kind that nobody else is chasing. The kind that doesn't come from some overpriced lead generation service with a hundred other investors already circling. You need deals that are off-radar. Hidden in plain sight. That's where the real money is.

Now, people ask me all the time, "Logan, where do you find these distressed properties?" And I always tell them the same thing. It's not about being fancy. It's about being smart. You don't need to spend thirty thousand a month on PPC ads. You don't need to buy every software subscription under the sun. You don't need a call center in the Philippines or a marketing funnel that looks like a NASA mission plan.

What you need is a dang delinquent tax list.

That's it.

Let me be clear—almost every distressed property we've ever bought started out the same way. It was on a tax delinquency list. We didn't scrape five different data providers and Frankenstein a master list. We didn't chase probate code violations or expired listings. We called the dadgum tax list. That's how simple this gets. Now, not all tax lists are created equal. Some counties make it easy. Others make it a maze. But I'm telling you right now, it's worth the effort. If you want to get into this game without breaking the bank, the delinquent tax list is your golden ticket. It's public record, and in most counties, you can either download it online or request it directly from the tax office.

The funny part is, when we started doing this, I assumed everyone was doing it. I figured every smart investor must be pulling the same list and calling the same folks. But I was dead wrong. Most people either don't know about it, or they're too lazy to do the work. They want push-button real estate. They want the leads to come to them. That ain't how this works.

Here's what we learned after a couple of years of running the business strictly off these lists: almost every big profit deal we did had one thing in common. The property had unpaid taxes. Didn't matter if it was land, a teardown house, a warehouse, or even a half-built subdivision. If the owner stopped paying taxes, that meant there was distress. That meant a conversation was worth having. But let me back up and explain why this list matters so much.

Delinquent taxes aren't just a red flag. They're a full-blown flare in the night sky. When someone falls behind on their taxes, it's not because they forgot. It's because they don't care about it or don't want the property any longer, or simply, they don't have any business owning real estate. That's a clear indicator of financial distress. And financial distress always leads to motivation—eventually. Not always quickly, but certainly.

Now, a lot of folks make the mistake of calling people after the first year of delinquency. But that's usually too early. I've been broke before. I know how that game goes. You fall behind on something, and at first, you lie to yourself. You say you'll catch up next month. You'll borrow from your cousin. You'll work some overtime. You make excuses.

But as the months pass and the bills pile up, reality sets in. By year two or three, that tax bill has ballooned, the county is filing lawsuits, and the seller starts to get more realistic. The games are over. That's when you get the deal.

So we filter our list. I don't want the ones who are just a few months behind. I want the ones who are two to three years behind. In Bexar County, where I do a lot of my work in South TX large cities, we've got a tax rate of just under three percent. That means if someone has a house worth three hundred grand, and owes thirty grand in back taxes, they've been ignoring that bill for a long time.

And by the time they're that deep in the hole, they're usually ready to talk. They're not hanging on to hope anymore. They've come to grips with the fact that they can't fix this. That's when the real conversations begin. And that's where we live.

We've pulled every type of lead list you can imagine. Pre-foreclosures, probate, water shutoffs, code violations, inherited property lists, bankruptcy court filings. We've done it all. But when we went back and looked at the data, one thing stood out. The tax list beat everything else. Not just in volume, but in profitability. The biggest, baddest, messiest, highest-margin deals all came from delinquent tax leads.

And here's the part that shocks people. We close multiple six- and seven-figure deals every year using a lead source that costs us less than a thousand bucks for 3 lists. That's not marketing fluff. That's real. You could literally build a million-dollar acquisition pipeline off a few hundred dollars and some sweat equity.

You don't need to over-engineer this. You don't need to become a professional data scientist. You need a spreadsheet with some delinquent properties, a decent skip trace, and a willingness to pick up the phone and make the call.

That's what separates the folks who make it in this business from the ones who flame out. It's not software. It's not branding. It's not having the best CRM. It's discipline. It's consistency. It's being willing to work leads nobody else wants to touch.

And once you get someone on the phone? You listen. You ask good questions. You let them tell you the story. And nine times out of ten, if they're behind on taxes, there's more going on beneath the surface. Maybe the house is in probate. Maybe the family's fighting over it. Maybe there's an old loan nobody can track down. Breaks in the title chain. Maybe unreleased liens. That's where the margin lives. Inside those problems.

So don't fall into the trap of chasing shiny object lead sources. Don't spend 30 grand a month trying to get warm PPC leads like everyone else. Call the people nobody else is calling. The ones with real distress. The ones with real pain. The ones who need help, not just a high offer.

That's where I built this business. That's where I still live today.

CHAPTER NINE

WHAT I ACTUALLY SAY TO SELLERS

How I Talk to People to Get Deep Discounts Without Lying

Let me tell you something that might surprise a few folks who've been taught the classic "hard close" real estate scripts. I don't run high-pressure sales calls. I'm not some fast-talking, objection-handling machine trying to manipulate people into signing a deal. That's not me. Never has been.

What I do is have honest conversations with people who have a problem. I ask questions. I listen. And then I tell them the truth. That's it.

If you can't talk to people, this business is going to be really hard for you. You'll get eaten alive in this space if you treat every conversation like it's some kind of one-call close or if you think you can just "script" your way through difficult situations. Distressed sellers aren't stupid. They're dealing with some heavy shit—death in the family, years of unpaid taxes, legal battles, bankruptcies, liens, all of it. They can smell fake a mile away.

So I don't try to trick them. I don't make fake promises. And I sure as hell don't pretend like I'm doing charity work. I just tell them how it is.

Let me give you an example of how one of these conversations goes down. I'll pick up the phone, and it usually sounds like this: "Hey there, I saw your name pop up on a property over on West Martin. I'm a real estate guy in the area, and I take on the big projects most can't fix, the ones that have big title problems, your property looks like one that I do, would you mind having a conversation to see if it's a good fit for me and the legal team?

Simple. That's it. No fluff, no pitch. I'm just trying to see if there's even a conversation to be had.

Sometimes they say, "Hell no, I'm keeping it." Okay, cool. I move on. But more often than not, they say something like, "I've thought about it," or, "I've been meaning to do something with it." That's when I started asking questions. I'm not trying to pounce. I just want to know what's going on.

And here's where the magic happens—not in my sales skills, but in my curiosity. I'll say things like:

"If you don't mind me asking, what's keeping you from selling it so far?"

"Are you the only person on title, or are there other family members involved?" It looked like a whole soccer team of folks share title with you.

"Have you tried listing it before, or was there something that made that tough, there are a million things that can keep property from selling but me and the legal department normally can fix it."

What I'm doing is digging into the problem without making them feel like they're being interrogated. I'm not shoving a contract down their throat. I'm listening. And when people feel heard, they start to open up. They start to tell you the real story. And man, once you know the story, you know the path to the deal.

Now here's the part where most investors screw this up. They start trying to sell themselves. They go into this spiel about how they pay cash, close fast, and blah blah blah. Sellers have heard it all before. That's not what gets deals done.

What gets deals done is being straight after identifying what the problem is, and verifying that they are interested in selling. I tell people flat-out:

"Look, I'm gonna be honest with you. I'm not gonna be your highest offer. In fact, I might be your lowest. But I'm the guy who can actually close. I'm the guy who knows how to solve the problem. If you want retail, I'm not your guy. But if you want out of the mess and you want it handled, I'm the guy." I can't promise you I'll fix the problems if I buy it, but I can buy it with those problems so they aren't yours anymore.

I let them know that I'm going to make money. And I tell them why. "I'm going to make good money if I get this deal done. If I screw it up, I might lose money. But here's what I know: this is a problem property. You wouldn't still have it if it was easy to sell. Realtors cannot or don't want to touch it. You've probably had other people make you offers and disappear. I'm not that guy. I'll close. But I can't pay top dollar for it. It's gonna take a lot of work on my end to get it there."

You know what happens when I say that?

They respect it.

They don't always say yes on the spot, but they don't slam the phone down either. A lot of them say, "I appreciate your honesty." And then a few days later, they call back. Or they sign the contract. Because they've been dealing with so much BS, hearing someone actually tell them the truth is a relief. Also, no one else can buy messes like this so I'm usually the only option in their market. It's me or no one.

Now look—I don't want to gloss over something important here. You have to know what you're talking about. You can't just talk a good game. You actually have to know how to clean up the title, solve liens, figure out probate issues, track down missing owners, negotiate payoffs, and all of that. You can't bluff your way through that stuff. If you say you're going to solve their problem, you'd better be ready to do it.

But assuming you've done the work or have a team behind you that can, then your job is to communicate that clearly and calmly to the seller. The more you learn how to explain what's going on with their property, the more deals you'll close.

Here's what I mean: You've got to tell people what their problem is before they even understand it themselves.

Like this:

"So based on what you're telling me, sounds like the property is still in your dad's name, and he passed away a few years ago. That's probably why the title is tied up. So what that means is we'd have to get the probate alternative work done in order before anyone could sell it. If you've got siblings, we'd need their signatures too. Also likely have judgments to liens to strip. That's not hard, but it's why the house hasn't sold yet. It's a mess. I can clean it up, but I've got to make sure the price makes sense because it's gonna take time and money." Usually, each deal I do has a $26-20K legal budget, you usually need some legal support to get to the finish line.

You explain it like that, and people start to get it. They realize you're not just a cash buyer, you're a problem solver. And that's what they're looking for.

So if you're wondering what to say on the phone—don't memorize a script. Learn the problems. Learn how to explain them. Learn how to show sellers what's really going on with their property. And then be honest about what it's going to take to fix it.

That's what I do. Every single day. And it's made me tens of millions.

CHAPTER TEN

THE PAPERWORK THAT PROTECTS ME

Options Contracts, Purchase Agreements, and How I Structure Deals Safely

You want to know a big thing that helps what separates the amateurs from the pros in this game? It ain't how many cold calls they make in a day. It's not how fancy their CRM is or how cool their Instagram looks. It's how well they protect themselves when they get a deal on the hook. Because here's the truth—if you can't structure a deal right, you're walking into a minefield.

When I first started in this business, I made some mistakes. We all do. I didn't have the right paperwork, I didn't know the timelines I should be giving myself, and I didn't understand how to legally protect my time, money, or the opportunity. I got burned. Learned some tough lessons. But I made it a point real quick: if I'm going to operate in this messy, unpredictable, distressed property world, I need to know my contracts inside and out—and I need to use the right ones for the right situation.

So let's talk about what I use today, how I use it, and how you can keep your ass covered when a deal turns sideways.

Why I Use Option Contracts First

Early on, I realized something: a lot of folks in this business rush to get a signed contract because they're excited to have something under contract. I get that—it feels good. But that excitement can turn into a disaster if you sign something too fast and find out the deal's got more landmines than you thought.

That's why I usually start with an **option contract**.

An option contract is not the same as a full-blown purchase agreement. It's basically an agreement that says, "I'll pay you this small amount—say $10 or $100—for the right, but not the obligation, to buy your property at this agreed price within a certain period of time." It gives me control without committing me to close. That's huge. In the distressed world, far more so than traditional real estate, you need the seller's commitment so I can spend valuable time and money on the due diligence on the seller to property's problems to determine if the juice is worth the squeeze.

Why?

Because I'm not buying a turnkey house in a gated neighborhood with a clear title and a smiling seller. I'm buying garbage. I'm buying properties with liens, broken families, lawsuits, busted roofs, and 20-year-old code violations. I'm buying from people who sometimes don't even fully own the house.

So what I want is time. I need breathing room to run the title, find all owners, check the value, and make sure this deal is real. The option contract gives me that. It keeps the seller from shopping the deal around, but it doesn't lock me into buying something that turns out to be a pile of trouble.

I usually give myself a **10-day option period** and a 5-**10-day close after that**, so I've got 40 days total. That's more than enough time to get my arms around the problem, figure out if it's fixable, and make sure I'm not stepping into a legal or financial mess. The funny thing is generally I actually close in 2-3 days, but want time in case I need it.

And if I find out the problems are bigger than I expected? I walk. That's the beauty of the option.

When I Go Hard on a Deal

The option expires and the contract goes "hard" on the commitment to buy the property. Now, if I get into the deal and everything checks out, or if I already know the situation and feel confident from day one, I'll use a standard **purchase and sale agreement**. This is the full contract that commits both sides to a closing.

But I want to be clear—I don't use some janky, two-page contract I found on a Facebook group.

In Texas, we've got a real estate commission (TREC) that puts out a standardized contract. It's the one that brokers, realtors, judges, and title companies are all familiar with. If you're in another state, your local board will have something similar. That's the one you use, but I do use a 5-page custom contract at times, again not from a FB group, its been built to and revised by my attorney over the years.

Why use promulgated forms?

Because everyone understands it. Nobody questions it. And in a dispute, the court, lawyers, mediators, and most folks already know how to read it.

I don't care if you're brand new or have been in the game for a decade—**use the forms everyone knows** until you're seasoned enough to understand how and why to modify them. We've got our own custom contracts now, but that came after hundreds of deals and a whole lot of legal review.

The standard contract has all the right terms: earnest money, inspection period, closing date, assignment clause, title contingencies, etc. The one biggest clause I care about? The **inspection period** (which functions like my second option) functions as a safety net for me.

Earnest Money: You Don't Need a Fortune

Now people always ask me, "How much earnest money do I need?" The answer is: **not much**.

I've locked up million-dollar properties with $100 in earnest money. You'd be surprised how often sellers don't care what that number is—as long as you're confident and clear in what you're doing. And title companies are fine with it too, especially on distressed deals. That said, I try to stick to 1% of purchase money because it looks better when reviewed by 3rd party, or if heaven forbid a judge has to read it. Shows I'm vested.

The point of earnest money isn't to "prove" anything—it's just a way to memorialize the contract. It's symbolic in these types of deals, it's a good faith deposit showing buyer is serious by posting funds.

So don't let some guru convince you that you need to put up $5 or $10 on every deal. You shouldn't. Especially when you're operating in such a unique and messy business. Do things right and stand behind it, even if you wind up in court.

Why I Never Overpromise

Another thing I learned early: **don't make promises you can't keep.** If you tell a seller, "I'm going to pay you $80,000 and we'll close in seven days," and then you realize the title is a dumpster fire, now you've lost credibility. They'll talk to someone else. They'll badmouth you to their cousin who owns five other properties. They'll back out. You lose.

Instead, I keep it real. I say:

"Here's the deal. I want to buy your property. But before I can close, I've got to get some research done unless you can answer all the questions and we've got to work through a few things. If it turns out to be manageable, I'll close quickly. But if we hit bumps, it could take a few weeks. I'll keep you posted the whole time."

That sets expectations. It gives me flexibility. And most importantly—it builds trust. Sellers can deal with a delay if they know you're still working and you haven't ghosted them. What they can't deal with is silence and broken promises.

How I Use Assignments and JVs the Right Way

Now, I don't wholesale really. Most of what I do, I actually close on. And sometimes if it makes sense. Lots of folks find these deals and I can't fix them, but we partner for a shave of profit and clean the deal so it can close.

If you're using an option or a purchase agreement, **make sure your contract lets you assign** it. That's what gives you flexibility. But more importantly, make sure you disclose everything to your seller. I tell them straight up:

"Look, I'm going to be honest with you. The buyer brought me in as a partner on this deal. If I do, we'll still handle everything for you, and nothing changes on your end. But I like to keep things transparent." We're the experts and will have the best shot at solving this for y'all. Then again, I'm transparent about the fact that I stand to earn handsomely if I do solve it.

That little sentence right there has saved me more headaches than I can count. Because if the seller finds out you made 80 grand flipping their property and you never mentioned it, they get angry. But if you tell them upfront, even if they don't fully understand the mechanics, they respect you. And that respect is what keeps deals together.

Close the Loop

To wrap this chapter up, I'll just say this: your paperwork isn't just about getting the deal done. It's about **keeping the deal alive when things get messy**, and **protecting your ass when people start asking questions**.

Start with an option contract if there's any doubt. Most times your state's standard purchase agreement works, and goes hard on the contract. When you're ready to move forward. Keep your earnest money reasonable. Be honest about your process. And never sign anything you don't understand.

You're not in this business to look busy—you're here to get rich solving problems. However, solving problems requires structure. The right contracts are what give you that structure.

Get good at this part, and you'll sleep better at night—and your deals will run a hell of a lot smoother.

Let me know when you're ready to keep rolling.

Chapter Eleven is next—where I'll walk you through how I actually **run title, identify problems, and break deals down like a forensic accountant.** It's where most investors give up... but where we start getting paid.

RUNNING TITLE LIKE A FORENSIC ACCOUNTANT

How I Dig into Ownership, Liens, Lawsuits, and the Land-mines That Can Blow Up a Deal

I tell people all the time—**that distressed property is not about houses.** It's about **paperwork, problems, and people.** Many times I say we're in the people business and we trade in real estate. Do you think you're buying a three-bedroom house on the south side? You're not. You're buying a tangled web of missed payments, legal history, ownership messes, bankruptcies, divorces, judgments, and whatever else that property's been through over the last 20 to 100 years. And if you don't know how to run the title and investigate that history, you're not just guessing—you're gambling. It's not that hard, you can learn on YouTube in a few days, or you can buy a 3rd party title report, countless providers exist online for $200!

I've seen wholesalers get a property under contract, find a buyer, and then right before closing—boom—title report shows up with a $200K IRS lien or a $50K credit card judgment and suddenly everybody's pretending they didn't see it coming. That's amateur hour. If you want to get paid consistently in this space, you need to learn how to **read title like a detective** and **ask the right questions before anyone else even realizes there's a problem.** Additionally, searching the owner of record and all other owners in the more recent ownership history can reveal a land mine of judgments/liens that also need to be addressed.

So let me walk you through how I do it.

Don't Wait for the Title Company—Do Your Own Recon Early

First off, don't sit around waiting for the title company to do your work for you. They'll get you a title commitment when they're ready, and that's great. But in this business, time is the one currency you can't get back. So I get to work **immediately.**

The first place I go? **The county's appraisal district and the county clerk's office.** Most of this is online now—most every county has a public-facing records search, and it doesn't take a genius to learn how to use it.

If I've got a name, a property address, I can start building a picture in 20 minutes. I look at:

- **The deed history** – Who bought it and when? Has it changed hands recently? Was it inherited? Quitclaimed? Was a will the conveyable instrument and not a deed? They're like that.
- **The liens and abstracts** – Are there IRS liens, judgment liens, mechanics' liens, old unreleased mortgages

or renovation loans, child support? These things don't just disappear.

- **Open mortgages** – How many? When were they taken out? Are they paid off? Are they in default?
- **Probate or deceased owner clues** – If the owner is dead, is there a will? Did it go through probate? Are there other heirs?

I'm piecing together a timeline—like a forensic accountant, but for dirt.

Ask the Seller the Right Questions—But Verify Everything

Now don't get me wrong, I talk to the seller too. I ask:

- "Do you have a mortgage?"
- "Is it current?"
- "Any other debts tied to the property?"
- "Did you inherit this, or buy it yourself?"
- "Was there a divorce, a death, a lawsuit?"
- "What do I need to know that I don't currently?"

But here's the deal—I don't **rely** on their answers. Not because they're lying, always, but because most people genuinely don't know. They think the mortgage was paid off, but they're wrong. They think the house is in their name, but it never got transferred. They think their cousin doesn't have a claim, but he does.

So I verify. Every time. Because this is real estate, and **what you don't know will hurt you.**

Red Flags I Watch For on Every Deal
Here are a few things that, when I see them, I slow way down:

1. **Bankruptcies** – If the seller ever filed bankruptcy, that property might be part of the estate—even if they say it's not. That means the bankruptcy trustee may have a say, or the title company may require court documentation.

2. **Multiple liens** – If I see a second mortgage, an HOA lien, and a couple of judgments, I'm reading the statute cheat sheet calling before I move another inch. Some of those can be negotiated or wiped, but some are sticky and require releases or settlements.

3. **Old private mortgages or weird investor notes** – These pop up more than you think, especially if the property was seller-financed in the past. Sometimes those lenders are dead. Sometimes they're companies that dissolved years ago. You'll need creative strategy or legal help to clean them up.

4. **Heirs on title** – If the last deed is to a person who's now deceased, and no probate has been filed, buckle up. You're going to need to find heirs, get affidavits, and possibly open probate. It can be done, but it ain't fast.

5. **Active lawsuits** – If the county docket search shows a recent lawsuit involving the property or seller, hit the brakes. That can stall or kill a deal depending on what it's about. On the bright side, those are opportunities that join the fund, and merge the litigations to benefit your seller if the seller agrees to the right prize to make it worth your time. Ask me how I know.

I've had deals with **child support liens that followed a seller across three counties, deeds where the notary wasn't licensed, probates where one of the heirs is in prison**, and **properties that changed hands three times without ever filing a deed.** All of that is solvable—**if you find it early.**

Building Your Title Muscles

Now, look—I'm not saying you need to become a lawyer or a title underwriter. But you do need to **know enough to spot the red flags**, ask smart questions, and partner with the right people to fix them. That's what professionals do.

Here's what I recommend:

- Spend time in your local county records portal. Just search random addresses. Get used to reading deeds and lien documents. The language is boring, but it's your armor in this game.

- Learn how to pull a title chain. It's usually just a series of deed filings and transactions that let you follow ownership back in time.
- Build relationships with **title officers** who know investment deals. Not all title companies understand creative finance, inherited property, or distressed stuff. Find one who does, and treat them like gold.
- If you're in Texas, get good at using county property records search tools, docket searches, and tax delinquency lookups.

This knowledge isn't flashy. It doesn't look cool on Instagram. But it's the reason I get deals others walk away from. And it's the reason I get paid big while other folks spin their wheels.

If You Want the Deal, You've Got to Own the Problem

At the end of the day, the reason these deals are available at such steep discounts is **because they're messy.** And most people run when things get complicated.

I run toward the fire.

I don't always have all the answers up front. But I know how to dig, how to learn, how to ask the right people for help. And most importantly, I know how to bring a deal together when everyone else gave up.

Because here's the thing—**you don't get rich from clean properties. You get rich from chaos.** And the only way to profit from chaos is to master it.

This chapter was about title. But what I'm really teaching you is how to think like an investigator. How to follow the paper trail, connect the dots, and solve the puzzle faster than the next guy. You do that well, and you'll never be short on deals.

Ready for **Chapter 12**? That's where I'll break down **how I talk to sellers in messy situations**—the language I use, the stories I tell, and the psychology that makes people trust me when their backs are against the wall. Let me know, and I'll keep going.

CHAPTER TWELVE

TALKING TO SELLERS IN THE MIDDLE OF A FIRE

How to Earn Trust, Lower Resistance, and Get Them to Say Yes (Even in a Mess)

The biggest mistake I see new folks make is thinking this game is about data. Or systems. Or lists. Or cold calls. Don't get me wrong—those things matter. But if you want to win in this business? I mean really win?

You better learn how to talk to people who are in trouble.

Because that's what distressed real estate is. It's not just beat-up houses or vacant lots or abandoned warehouses,—it's a person on the other end of the line who's drowning in legal bills, behind on taxes, getting calls from creditors, maybe even fighting with family over a property no one wants to deal with.

If you come at that seller with slick sales tactics, big promises, or high-pressure nonsense, you'll get nowhere. I don't care how good your contract looks. You might as well throw it in the trash. Because distressed sellers—real distressed sellers—**can smell**

bullshit from a mile away. I've said this a few times, make sure it sinks in.

So in this chapter, I'm going to walk you through exactly how I talk to sellers. How I build trust. How I listen. How I help them sort through the mess. And how I earn the right to get that contract signed.

Rule #1: Come in Low, Come in Calm

When I call a seller, I don't open with a sales pitch. I don't open with numbers. I don't even tell them who I am right away. I come in low and calm. I might say:

"Hey, this is Logan. I know this is out of the blue, but I was calling about that lot on South Main St. I saw your name attached to it and wasn't sure if you still owned it or if I even had the right person. Are you even the right call? Mind if I ask a couple of questions?"

See what I did there? It's conversational. It's uncertain. It's casual. That makes people **lean in**, not put their guard up. I'm not certain up front so I want to act that way. I give them a shot at helping me out, and most times they will.

I let the conversation happen. I don't press. I don't pitch. I don't act like I'm here to change their life. I'm just a guy calling to ask a question about a property.

That's how you start building trust.

Rule #2: Find the Real Problem

Once I confirm I'm talking to the right person, I start peeling the layers back.

"Has that property been in your family a long time?"

"Are taxes still behind on it?"

"Looks like there may have been a lien or two—have y'all tried to sell it before?"

These aren't interrogations. I'm not rapid-firing them. I'm listening, responding, and letting them talk. I want them to talk 70% of the call or more. I nurture and guide the call and only share information at times. This model establishes consistency and trust. It just does.

Sometimes I'll ask:

"Why haven't y'all sold it before now?"

And man, let me tell you—**this question is magic.** Because it gets people to open up about all the stuff they've been hiding or avoiding.

You'll hear everything from:

- "It's not in my name. My uncle left it to us, but he never did a will."
- "We tried, but the city keeps telling us there are code issues."
- "We don't talk to my sister anymore, so we can't get her to sign off on it."

Now you've got your story. Now you know where the mess is. And once you know the mess, you can start talking about solutions.

Rule #3: Tell Them the Truth About What You Do

Here's something that'll surprise people—I don't hide what I do. At all. I tell them straight up:

"Look, I'm not a charity. If I can buy this, fix the issues, and resell it, there's a good chance I'll make some real money. But there's also a chance it's worse than it looks, and I might lose money. It's hard to say until I get into it. All I can do is shoot straight with you and tell you what I think is possible." I also advocate to them that I'm not someone buying their property but taking their place in a bad situation to hope to solve it. Frames the matter better.

That honesty disarms people. Because let's face it, they're used to getting cold calls from wholesalers who don't know the first thing about property code or tax law but are promising cash in 10 days. The seller knows that's not real. They feel it, or they have already tried and been let down multiple times. My goal is to identify that to differentiate me for it.

When I tell them what I really do—buy problem properties, clean them up, and flip them for a profit—I get respect. When I walk them through the mess and explain what it'll take to fix it, I get trust. Even more trust is earned when I explain to them how they can drift or move sales prices, but I'm here if you don't want to. And when you have someone's trust, you can get a deal done.

Rule #4: Lower Their Expectations—Then Exceed Them

A lot of new investors feel pressure to impress sellers. They promise fast closings, big checks, and simple processes. And when things get hard—as they always do with distressed deals—the seller gets pissed.

That's why I take the opposite route.

I tell people:

"Look, this won't be fast. It won't be easy. And it might not even be possible. But I'll give it an honest effort and keep you posted every step of the way." "I've also solved more of these than any one operation, so thermos I'm your best shot"

When you do that, and then you *actually perform*—you find the cousin, you pay the lien, you get the title cleared, and you close—that seller thinks you're a damn miracle worker.

You know what they do then?

They tell their neighbors. They tell their family. They bring you more deals.

I've gotten deals handed to me simply because I was the only person who didn't sugarcoat the process.

Rule #5: Keep It Human

Last but not least, you've got to remember—**this is a human business.** These are real people with real lives, real mistakes, real pain. You're not just solving a real estate problem. You're solving a *life* problem.

Sometimes that means helping them relocate. Sometimes that means helping them talk to a lawyer. Sometimes it means buying them groceries while they wait for the deal to close.

Do you think that's above your pay grade?

Then this isn't the business for you.

But if you can show up, listen, understand the situation, and bring real solutions without pressure or judgment—you'll do just fine. Because these folks need someone who will tell them the truth and guide them out of the mess.

Be that person, and the deals will come.

Next up is **Chapter 13**, where I'll get into how we evaluate these properties without ever stepping foot on them—how we estimate value, determine exit strategy, and price our offers to win. This is a missing puzzle piece for most, I'll keep rolling, so listen up!

CHAPTER THIRTEEN

RUNNING THE NUMBERS WITHOUT EVER LEAVING YOUR CHAIR

How I Value Distressed Property Without a Tape Measure, from my desk

One of the most common questions I get from folks—especially newer investors—is, "Logan, how the hell do you know what to offer on these properties if you're not even going to see them in person?"

And I get it. We've all been taught that real estate is local, boots-on-the-ground, belly-to-belly. They say you gotta walk it, smell it, shake the neighbor's hand, and imagine the remodel in your head. And that's all fine and good—for someone flipping houses or doing traditional acquisitions. That's easy for slim-margin deals because they are too easy to botch.

But this business I'm in? The one I've built from the ground up over ten years? That's not what we do here. Because when you're dealing with distressed assets—especially the kinds of messy, tangled-up title-nightmare properties I go after—**you don't need granite countertops and a nice floorplan.**

What you need is margin. And that starts with **a smart, conservative valuation process** you can run from a laptop, sitting in your truck or at the kitchen table. An old retired wealthy investor once told me "There is no bad product, only bad pricing!" it's foundational to let me show you exactly how I do it. My business now!

We Don't Talk ARV in My Office

First off, let me make something crystal clear: **ARV is a dirty word in my office. In the real estate investing world ARV means After Repair Value.**

If I hear someone walk in talking about, "Well the ARV is $280K and I think we can get it for $170K," I stop them right there. Because that's not how we do business.

ARV assumes construction. It assumes remodel. It assumes risk and time and execution—all things I want no part of if I can help it.

I don't care what it could be worth after a $70,000 rehab.

I care what it's worth today.

As-is. With problems. With trash in the yard and no utilities on. With an open code case and a broken fence.

That's the number that matters.

Because that's the number I can sell it for tomorrow. That's the number I can underwrite. That's the number I can protect myself with. So we start there—**what it's worth as-is, right now.**

Where I Get My Values (Hint: It's Not Fancy)

Now this part's going to surprise a lot of people, especially if they're used to hearing folks pitch software subscriptions and fancy valuation tools.

Here's the truth:

I use two websites:

- The County Appraisal District
- Redfin (sometimes Realtor.com, depending on the market) or Zillow, pick your favorite of the retail vacation sites.

That's it.

I go to the CAD to see what the county thinks it's worth. Now look, counties don't always get it right—sometimes they under-value, sometimes they over value—but more often than not, it gives me a baseline. It shows me what the market thinks it was worth last year. More or less, order of magnitude value.

Then I hop on Redfin and pull up sold comps—**not listings, not pendings, but closed deals.** I'm looking for nearby sales of similar size, similar lot types, and similar level of condition *if I can find it.* Let's say the appraisal district says $170K. Redfin shows three recent comps at $220K, $185K, and $190K. I'll usually average them out—maybe call it $190K conservatively—and then chop a bit off for good measure.

Because remember: **we are not retail buyers.** We're not paying full price. We're buying at a discount, solving a problem, and reselling quickly. So our valuation has to be pessimistic by design.

The Delta is What Keeps You Safe

Once I've got my conservative as-is value—let's say it's $190K—I back into what I'd want to pay.

And I'll tell you what my goal is every time: **I want to be between 10 and 50 cents on the dollar. The more ready the owner is to get rid of the problem, the lower on the 10 cents to 50 cents scale my officer is.**

If I can get that $190K property for $95K, that's okay. If I can get it for $70K, even better. But if I'm paying $130K or $140K? I better have a damn good reason. Because that's too thin for a messy deal.

The bigger that delta—the spread between what I pay and what I can list it for—the more mistakes I can make and still come out ahead. Here I'm trying to have a margin of safety, to protect capital, and no matter what goes wrong, I won't risk capital.

If I overpay for a haul-off? No big deal.

If I find out later there's a code violation that takes three months to clear? Still okay.

If a cousin comes out of the woodwork and we have to renegotiate ownership interest? I've got a cushion.

That's why this model works. It's not that I'm smarter than everybody else. It's that I'm buying with a buffer.

Quick Case Study: $48,000 In, $194,000 Out

Let me give you a real number to chew on. I ran a report in my office last year—took the last 100 properties we bought and ran the averages, out of one of the business lines.

The **average acquisition price was $48,000.** That's what we spent to buy the deal—purchase price, legal fees, lien payoffs, everything. The **average sales price was $194,000.** That's what we resold them for on the open market. No ARV. No remodel. No heavy construction. Just cleaned up, cleared title, and listed.

So our gross margin was roughly $150,000. After closing costs, commissions, and overhead, our net margin was in the $125,000 range.

You show me a flipper doing that kind of margin on a $48K spend, and I'll eat my words.

But you won't find many. Because this model—**buying problems, solving them, and reselling clean title on the open market**—is more efficient than anything else I've seen in real estate. He $200k price point closet seemed so glamorous, small capitalization, but net profit and net returns are astounding. I've found nothing comparable in the small cap real estate space.

You Don't Have to Be a Genius

Here's the best part. You don't have to be a genius to do this.

If you can read the county appraisal value, look up some comps on Redfin, and run some quick math in a notepad, you can make solid decisions.

Hell, in the beginning, I did it all with pen and paper, knocking on doors in San Antonio. You don't need a $10,000 mentorship or a $300/month CRM to figure this out. That mentorship may help you connect the dots faster, but if I figured it out on my own, you could too. I run a mentorship program for serious operators who don't want to talk forever to figure the business out, in four months.

You need good instincts. Conservative numbers. And the discipline to walk away from deals that don't pencil. Don't fall in love with the deal or get a deal. A saying I love is "The best deal I ever did, was the one I didn't do.

Because if you mess up your valuation on a flip, you can lose your shirt. If you overpay on a rental, you might break even. But if you stay disciplined in this model—only buy when there's blood in the streets—or extreme distress in the air. You'll almost never lose.

Up next is **Chapter 14**, where I'll show you exactly what we do after we get a property under contract—how we solve the mess, clear title, and get it to market without ever swinging a hammer. Lets go, lets keep pushing forward.

CHAPTER FOURTEEN

SOLVING THE MESS:

HOW WE TURN A BROKEN DEAL INTO A CLOSED ONE

You Don't Need a Toolbox of Tools, You Need a Toolbox of People

Once we've got a property under contract—and remember, we're talking the kinds of deals that are *hairy*, with problems all over the place—the real work starts. See, a lot of people think the acquisition is the hard part. Once you get the seller to sign, it's all downhill from there.

But that's where they're dead wrong. That's when our work starts. Because in this business, **you don't make your money at the close. You make it in the clean-up.** And I don't mean sweeping the floors—I'm talking title work, liens, judgments, legal issues, unknown owners, all of it. That's where the value gets created. And that's where most folks throw up their hands and walk away. That's why there's less competition. Because most investors don't want to deal with it.

But here's what I've learned: **you don't need to be the expert in everything—you just need to know what needs solving and who can solve it.**

Let's break this down piece by piece.

Title is King (And Often the Problem)

When we send a contract over to the title company, we're not crossing our fingers hoping it closes smoothly. Quite the opposite—we're expecting problems. We're anticipating roadblocks. And usually, we're right.

Maybe there's a mortgage that was never properly released. Maybe there's an old lien from 2007 that never got cleared. Maybe someone died ten years ago, and the property never went through probate. Maybe one of the heirs is missing in Louisiana and nobody's heard from them since 2011.

All of that is our job to fix. Most think that's title's job, its not. Title's job is to escrow and issue policies, but some escrow officers help curative work, to be nice, but don't forget that work is sellers job, not titles. As buyers we should handle it to make the deals actually happen. It's our value proposition.

Most investors run when title gets ugly. But me? I lean in. Because that's the signal that no one else will be willing to do the work. That's where the profit hides.

Now let me be clear. I'm not the one drafting affidavits or filing motions. But I've got the people. A good title company. A solid probate attorney. A damn good private investigator. If you don't have those folks in your corner, get on the phone and start finding them. **Because they are the difference between your contract being a "maybe" and your deal getting wired in full. I choose the best pro services, for example, I hire the best litigators in town, and my private investigator is a retired FBI. Find the best.**

Ownership Disputes: 70% of the Game

Let's say you're under contract with two people who claim to own the property. Everything seems smooth—until title comes back and says there are seven other owners you didn't know about. Guess what? That's normal.

I've had properties with **sixty-five owners.** That's not a typo. Six-five. A massive family inheritance that got passed around, ignored, and left to rot. And I didn't shy away from it—I **tracked them all down, one by one, paid them out individually, and closed it.** You know what I bought it for? $250,000. Do you know what it was worth when I was done? $1.25 million. $170K to sellers, 70K to delinquent taxes, $10K to legal, and it was done, now 17 took 9 months to clean up and 4 to sell, put a home run.

So don't panic when there are other owners. Just start making calls. Here's the key: **you treat every owner like they're the only one.** You call them. You listen. You ask how they ended up involved. You figure out what they want. And then you make a deal. I deal with them all in silos, no need to try and get them all to get along again, they proved that's too hard already, let's contract each one separately, to treat them with confidentiality separately.

If they're fighting with their siblings? Fine. Don't try to get them all in the same room. Work them one by one. Many times, they hate each other too much to work together, but they'll work with you. That's your edge. So is communication. I always ask those fighting family types to please don't punish me for the bad deeds of their family. I'm not them, I'm the new guy trying to fix that person's problems, I'm here with the white flag, is that ok? Very sensible, it works.

Liens, Judgments, Delinquent Taxes
You'll run into tax debt. You'll see IRS liens. You'll see code violations and demolition orders. It'll look scary. That's why these deals are cheap.
But here's the pro trick to manage your spending better: **you don't always have to pay it upfront.**
I've bought properties with $30,000 in back taxes and didn't pay them until the closing table like when I go to sell, the property on the back end. Yep, sort of subject to style. —because I negotiated it that way. We listed the property for $200,000, found a buyer, and let the title company use the buyer's funds to pay off the taxes and send me the net. That lowers my cash out of pocket along the way and juices my yield, by delaying some of the deb satisfaction until the disposition.
I was in that deal for $10,000 total. The seller got ten grand, and I made $140,000 profit—all because I understood how to structure the exit **after** solving the problem.

Option Contracts Buy You Time

I said this earlier, but it bears repeating: **do not promise fast closings unless you know for sure you can do it.**

Use option contracts. Give yourself some time days to solve the problem. Don't box yourself in.

And be honest with the seller. Say, "Look, I think I can help you, but there are a lot of moving parts. Here's how it works. I'm going to get you a simple contract that gives me the right to solve the issue and close this deal. If I can't do it, I walk. But if I can, you're going to get a check at the end."

That honesty builds trust. And that trust gives you space to work.

You Don't Need to Know Everything—You Just Need to Know How to Ask Questions

If you're reading all this and feeling overwhelmed, don't worry. That's normal. This business is full of weird legal stuff and edge cases. You won't know how to solve every problem at first. Hell, I still don't.

But what I *am* good at is asking questions and in the early days call lawyers and the title company and ask what's needed. I call the attorney and ask what the next step is. I call the seller and ask what they remember from 20 years ago. Today I know most of the solves after studying the property code, tax code, estates and probate code, and with years of functional experience.

I gather data. I push it forward. And I don't stop.
Most folks freeze up when the deal gets messy. I lean in. And because of that, I win deals others never even get close to.

From Problem to Profit

Let me leave you with this: every dollar I've made in this business came from solving someone else's problem.

I didn't get rich doing lipstick flips or cosmetic rehabs. I didn't build a portfolio by going to auctions. I didn't market to hundreds of thousands of people with postcards and ads.

I went straight to the mess.

I sat in the problems no one else wanted to deal with. I learned how to listen. I built a team that could help me fix things. And I learned how to **see value where others only saw risk.**

That's how we go from contract to close.

That's how we create wealth from thin air.

That's how you build a business that lasts.

Next up is **Chapter 15**, where we'll dive into what happens after the cleanup—how we list, price, and move property fast without leaving money on the table. Let me know when you're ready to roll forward.

Let's keep the momentum rolling with **Chapter 11** Grounded, transparent, and practical with a hell of a lot of detail. Here's where we talk about what happens after the mess is cleaned up, the title's clear, and it's time to actually **get paid.**

CHAPTER FIFTEEN

THE EXIT STRATEGY:

HOW WE MOVE INVENTORY FAST AND KEEP THE PROFITS TIGHT

Don't Fall in Love with the Property, Fall in Love with the Margin

Once we've wrestled through all the chaos—ownership disputes, delinquent taxes, busted title, old mortgage liens, and God knows what else—we finally get to the part that most investors think is the "easy" part: the resale.

Now I'll say this—it's definitely *easier* than tracking down 20 owners across four states. But don't get it twisted: how you handle the exit is just as critical as the acquisition and the cleanup.

Because this is where you can fumble a fat profit with one bad move. So let me walk you through how I handle exits, and more importantly, why we do it this way. Because most of y'all are used to wholesaling, flipping, or renting. And while this might look similar on the surface, we're not playing the same game. We're moving distressed inventory, and we treat it like a **retail product**, not a rehab project. It is inventory that needs to be quickly cycled and replaced. Here's where we bring liquidity to a less liquid asset, generally speaking.

We Sell Everything on the Market — Period

This is the first major difference between what I do and what a lot of investors are doing.

We don't wholesale these deals.

We don't assign the contracts.

We don't call up a flipper to take it off our hands. You can do all of those But I set up a process that works the same every time. The less customization the less you need to participate in that process after training some one else to do it for you.

We **buy the deal**, close on it ourselves, take title, and then we **list it on the MLS** with a licensed agent—just like a regular homeowner would.

Now I know some of y'all are thinking, "Wait, Logan—why wouldn't you just assign it and take a fast $10K?"

I'll tell you exactly why.

Because I didn't go through hell solving a decade of title issues and tracking down absentee owners in three states just to give the deal to someone else for peanuts. I already did the hard work. Why the hell would I leave all of the meat on the bone? I'll leave some so it sells quickly, but don't give up all the justice selling to the private market.

By listing the property, I get full retail exposure. I tap into the entire buyer pool. **Flippers, landlords, homeowners, develop-**

ers—everybody sees it. MLS buyers are usually repped by realtors who betted buyers and they are ready to move and are serious. No games and wasted time like usually with these new investor buyers via the wholesaler market.

And that's where we get the price up. But even more importantly—we get **speed**.

Price to Move — Never to Sit

When we price these properties, I don't look at ARV.

In fact, in my office, **ARV is a dirty word.** You say that around here, you're assigned to trash duty for the office for the week, or drop and give me 50 push ups, just don't say ARV in my office.

We price on **as-is value**—what it's worth today, without us lifting a hammer.

So if I've got a house that's beat to hell but in a decent area, and the comps say that after a full rehab it's worth $300,000, that means nothing to me. What matters is: what will someone pay for it **today**, as it sits?

That number might be $150,000. And if I'm into the deal for $70,000, then I know I've got a fat margin—and I don't need to hold out for top dollar.

So what do I do? I price it at $140,000.

You heard me right. I underprice it—**on purpose.** Not a lot, but enough to be interesting to drive traffic and attention to the listing. If I mess up and underprice too much, I'll get bid up and still won't leave money on the table. I'm here for the first 80% of the profit, the easiest part, not the last 20%. That part is exponentially harder to access.

Why? Because the goal isn't to hold a damn seminar for six months trying to squeeze out every dollar. The goal is to **move the deal**, recycle the capital, and do it again next week.

Every month a deal sits, it costs you money. Taxes, utilities, lawn care, insurance, opportunity cost—it all stacks up. Plus it clogs up your operation.

So if the as-is value is $150,000, I price it at $140,000, let the buyers fight over it, and take a clean offer with quick terms. Accept no options from buyers, hard earnest money. The best and most certain terms.

That's why our average days on the market is low. **We're pricing for speed, not ego.**

Four-Week Rule: If It Doesn't Sell, It's Overpriced

In my office, we have a hard rule: **if a property hasn't sold within 30 days, it's overpriced. Period.**

There's no "but the market's slow" or "it's a weird property" or "I think the right buyer just hasn't seen it yet."

Forget all that.

If it's not under contract in 4 weeks, we lower the price. Simple as that. Buyers vote with their checkbooks, and they're not confused. Either it's priced right or it's not. We don't make the price, or the value, that is mister markets job.

We don't fall in love with the property. We fall in love with the profit.

You don't go broke making $80,000 instead of $90,000. But you sure as hell can go broke chasing the extra 10 and letting the property sit for 4-6 months. Carrying cost to opportunity costs are far more expensive then most investors realize.

Sell It As-Is, Don't Touch a Thing

Let me make something really clear: **we don't rehab properties.** Not even a little.

We don't paint. We don't replace the carpet. We don't redo kitchens. We don't even patch holes in the drywall.

You know what we do?

We mow the grass. We trim the trees. We clean up the trash.

That's it. Just tidy it up for a nice presentation, make it simple to tour and see, and leave the heavy lift for the next guy.

Why? Because again—we're not trying to get top-dollar showroom pricing. We're not selling to someone who expects granite counters and stainless appliances.

We're selling to flippers, landlords, developers—**people who know what they're doing** and want a property they can put their own stamp on. They get to value add. I've found dollar per hour is much higher on paperwork than construction work. And when we clean it up and price it right, they show up ready to buy. Fast. And when we clean it up and price it right, they show up ready to buy. Fast.

Know Your Buyer Pool

When we list a property, we know exactly who we want as a buyer.

If it's a 2-bed 1-bath in a working-class neighborhood, we want a landlord.

If it's a lot downtown, we want a developer.

If it's a total teardown in a hot zip code, we want a flipper.

And we tailor our listing to speak to that person. We show the value. We give them the comps. We make it easy for them to see the opportunity. Today the AI tools make that so simple, so you have no excuse to get that one wrong.

That's what gets it sold.

The Exit is the Payoff—Don't Jam Yourself Up Before You Get There

Look, a lot of investors get 90% of the way through a deal and then make one bad decision that kills the return.

They overprice it.

They try to wholesale when they should've closed.

They promise rehab work they can't deliver.

They get greedy.

Don't do that.

You already did the hard part. You solved the title. You got the deal bought right. Don't fumble it in the red zone. Don't shit the bed, this is not an IQ problem, this is a commonsense problem. Get ahead of it and you will be handsomely rewarded.

Get it listed. Price it right. Let the buyer pool do its job. Markets are efficient, especially real estate markets in the USA, let it work for you, and don't overthink it.

And get that wire in the bank.

That's the game.

CHAPTER SIXTEEN

FROM HUSTLER TO OPERATOR:

TURNING THIS INTO A BUSINESS

A lot of folks get into this distressed property model the same way I did—part-time, chasing leads after work, doing your own research, making your own calls, trying to get that first deal to hit. It's just you, maybe a buddy, and maybe a VA if you're fancy. You're wearing ten hats and building the plane while you fly it. That's how it starts. But it's not where it ends. Sadly I see folk who entered the space with me 10 years ago and the game never evolved for them, they still do same thing the same way.

If you do it right—if you keep your head down, stay consistent, and learn how to solve real problems and improve the business year after year—you'll hit a point where you can't handle it all on your own. Deals will start coming in faster than you can process them. Money's coming in, but so are a bunch of headaches. Calls you forgot to return. Leads you didn't follow up on. Closings you had to reschedule because you were juggling too much.

That's the moment you need to decide: are you going to stay in **hustler mode**, or are you going to become an **operator**? A business omen.

Because there's a big damn difference between a self-employed deal chaser and someone running a real estate company that throws off real profit, month after month, with or without your hands on the wheel.

Let me show you what it takes to become that second guy.

Systems First, People Second

When people talk about scaling a business, they usually think about hiring people first.

But if you haven't built **systems**, all you're doing is hiring someone to step into your chaos. And that's what must do. That's before them without help but only overstep better, we want to ascend to the next floor, level, way up there.

I didn't hire a single person until I had my daily process mapped out—how leads came in, how they were tracked, how we followed up, how we sent contracts, how we solved problems, and how we disposed of the property. You've got to write this stuff down. It has to live somewhere **outside your head.**

We use Salesforce now. We also used Podio in the middle of excel and Salesforce. It's custom, robust, and designed for our workflow. But when I started, it was just a spreadsheet and some Google Docs. Whatever it is, make sure it's replicable. Because once the system's in place, then you can plug in the right people to run it.

That's when the income starts to tale on hokey stick growth. That is the game changer.

Hire Roles, Not Bodies

When it was finally time to bring people on, I didn't just go hire someone and tell them to "help out." That's a recipe for disaster. I hired for specific roles.

- One person was **acquisitions**—their job was to call leads, qualify them, and lock up contracts.
- One was an **admin**—handling paperwork, title submissions, coordination, and backend cleanup.
- One person was a **project manager**—managing clean outs, utility accounts, and repairs on the commercial portfolio I started to build.
- One person was a **bookkeeper** whose moving business needed fast-moving reports.

Everybody had a job. Nobody overlapped. That's how we stayed lean and efficient.

And the funny thing is, once you get two or three solid people in those seats, your capacity to do deals doesn't double—it **multiplies**.

Don't Scale the Wrong Things

This is one of the biggest lessons I learned the hard way. You don't scale expenses. You don't scale complexity.

You scale **execution**. I scaled what I was already dong and did not expand the scope one bit. Keep it simple and pour gas on the fire. S whole lot more of the same.

I didn't go drop $20,000 a month on PPC ads or build some giant VA team overseas. I scaled what already worked. I went deeper on delinquent tax leads. I refined my skip tracing. I got better at solving problems. I trained my team to think like I do. And we kept our overhead reasonable. We don't waste money just because we have it. If end dollar of spend doesn't increase efficiency big time or produce a yield, the money stays home.

That's the secret sauce: run lean, move fast, and only add complexity when the machine is too efficient to slow down.

Build a Company That Can Withstand a Bad Market

I've said this before, but it bears repeating—**a good market will cover your bad habits. A bad market will expose them all.**

When rates shot up post-pandemic and everyone was crying about the slowdown, our company didn't flinch. Why?

Because we buy at 10 to 50 cents on the dollar. We don't over-leverage. We don't run massive ad budgets. And we sell fast.

That model works in hot markets, cold markets, and sideways markets.

We didn't need to pivot. We were already positioned. We just washed, rinsed and repeated what we were already dong. We did lower prices to move inventory but with such low bases that was fine.

If you build your business right, it should be able to take a punch and keep swinging.

Lifestyle Business or Growth Engine? You Choose.

I've got guys in my office running 4 different kinds of companies, all using the same playbook. One of them does **one deal a month**, works 30 hours a week, and makes over a million dollars a year. He's got one assistant and a sales guy, and he's chill as it gets. That's a lifestyle business.

Another guy runs a **full-blown operation**—a team of four, heavy volume, big inventory, and more moving parts. He's pulling in eight figures in equity every year, but he works his ass off. That's a growth engine. The other two guys are somewhere in the middle of those two.

You get to choose what you build. This model supports both.

The important thing is, **that you build it intentionally.** Don't just build blindly. Don't try to copy someone else's business because it looks flashy. Build a company that fits your life.

And Most Important—Know Your Numbers

None of this matters if you don't know your numbers cold. I'm talking:

- Average purchase price
- Average resale price
- Days on market
- Cost per lead

- Average margin per deal
- Total capital in use
- Total equity in inventory
- Total overhead
- Overhead as % of revenue
- Overhead allocation per property
- EBITA

If you don't track that, you're not running a business—you're running a guessing game.

I check my financial reports every week. I know where the money is, where the bottlenecks are, and what to fix next.

That's what separates a hustler from an operator.

In **Chapter 17**, we're going to dig into the different ways to fund these deals. Because while I started off spending my own money, I quickly realized there's a better way—**other people's money, there's my money, there's credit.** Whether it's JV partners, private lenders, or creative deal structures, this model doesn't need your cash as much as it needs your skill.

Let's roll straight into **Chapter 17**, and now we're diving into the good stuff. Because if you're anything like I was in the beginning, you're probably thinking, "Logan, how the hell am I supposed to buy a house with 30 grand in back taxes when I don't even have five grand in the bank?" And I get that. I lived that. So this chapter is all about the truth behind **how to fund distressed deals without using millions of dollars from the start.**

CHAPTER SEVENTEEN

FUNDING THE RIGHT WAY:

WHY GOOD DEALS FIND THE MONEY

One of the biggest misconceptions in real estate—especially in distressed property deals—is that you need to have money to make money. Let me set the record straight right now: **you don't need to have capital. You need to have a good deal.**

Let me say that again, louder this time:

Good deals find money. Always.

That's not just a slogan. It's a reality I've lived over and over.

If you can find a $300,000 property and get it under contract for $80,000 because of a title mess or a probate issue or delinquent taxes, I don't care if you're dead broke—**there are twenty people lined up who will fund that deal in exchange for a cut.** And I'm one of them. In the early days I had more time and deals then money, so I also took on a partner to expand by injecting capital into the business. Thankfully he also helped me learn plenty of good business sense also. But the capital was the starting point.

You Only Need Two Things to Start

In the beginning, the only money I ever needed was:

1. A few grand for **earnest money**
2. A few bucks for **skip tracing or calling leads, well maybe a few hundred.**

That's it. I'm saying for less than $5K you can start.

Once I got a deal under contract, if I didn't want to fund it myself, I'd call someone like me—an investor who understands how valuable these distressed opportunities are—and say, "Hey, I got a contract. Want to partner?" then soon the partner I mentioned because full-time go-to.

Nine times out of ten, the answer was **hell yes**.

Because those of us who are liquid, we're looking for deals. We don't want to cold call or dig through probate files. We want folks like you bringing us contracts we can fund and make money on. That is the progression of your business hopefully. In the early days we have more time than money, but as things progress we begine to have more money than time, that is when we can start to invest in others.

You bring the deal. I bring the money. We both win. And you get your business and life off the ground.

The Power of Joint Ventures (JVs)

Some people act like JVs are a dirty word. They're not. They're how you go from struggling to making real money without debt. A **JV**, or Joint Venture, just means you're teaming up with someone—typically one person brings the deal, the other brings the funding, and you split the profits.

I've done hundreds of JV deals. Some of them were with folks who had never done a single deal before. They just followed the model I teach, got a seller to sign, and came to me for the rest. Do you want to know the crazy part?

Those first-timers made fifty, sixty, sometimes a hundred grand on their very first deal—without spending more than a couple hundred bucks total. Yes that's true. Mike Morris was a retired firefighter who's first deal vetted $320K which we split, from a $80K investment.

If that doesn't change your perspective on what's possible, I don't know what will.

What Do Investors Like Me Look For?

So, if you want someone like me—or one of my guys—to fund your deal, here's what you need:

- **One seller already talking.** Don't come to me with cold leads or "maybe I'll get them to call back." You need at least one party saying, "Yeah, I'd sell it."
- **A rough price worked out.** Doesn't have to be perfect.

But if the seller wants $80K and comps say it's worth $200K, I'm listening.

- **Some research**. I'm not asking for a title report, but know what you're looking at. Is it in probate? Are there taxes owed? How many owners got the basics and don't be too wrong?
- **A real shot at a big margin**. I'm not interested in chasing down ten owners for a $10,000 profit. But if the upside is $50K+, we'll throw bodies at it.

When you have that, you're not begging someone to fund your deal. You're offering them a profitable opportunity. There's a big difference.

Don't Chase Banks—Build Relationships

A lot of new investors waste time chasing **hard money lenders** or trying to qualify for traditional loans. Let me tell you right now, distressed property is not the playground for traditional financing.

- Banks hate uncertainty.
- Title issues scare lenders.
- Short option periods and seller drama don't play well with red tape.

So instead of chasing approval letters, **build relationships with people who understand this game.**

The money is in your network. Whether that's other real estate investors, flippers, attorneys, or even doctors with capital and no time—**you need to become the person who can turn their money into more money.**

Once people see you can take a $40,000 investment and turn it into $90,000 in a couple of months, you won't have to chase capital again. They'll chase you. In time you will grow your capital so that you don't need outside money, but until then plan for partner involvement.

Creative Structures That Work

Sometimes you don't need cash upfront at all. In fact, in a lot of our deals, we buy subject-to-existing liens or create seller financing structures. Let me give you some examples:

- **Subject-To the Taxes** – We buy the owner's interest for $10K, leave the taxes in place, and pay them off at closing when we resell. That could take ½ of a year, but preserves lots of capital.
- **Note** – We create a note and make a _____ Put and monthly payments to the seller, with a balloon payment in 6 months to 3 years pending project plan.
- **Options with Time** – Lock it up cheap, control the deal, then assign it or fund it later.

The key is: that you're controlling a high-margin asset for **pennies on the dollar**, and you're never over-leveraged because your entry point is so low.

This is chess, not checkers.

Look Like a Pro, Even If It's Your First Deal

When you approach a capital partner, don't come across like it's your first rodeo—even if it is.

Have your ducks in a row:

- Know what the property is worth (as-is, not ARV)
- Understand the seller's motivation
- Be honest about the challenges (title issues, multiple owners, liens, etc.)
- Explain the path to profit
- Have an estimate of the timeline.

And **don't pretend like you don't need them.** Just be clear: "I've got the deal. You've got the funds. Let's split it and win."

That confidence will carry you farther than any fake suit or polished pitch deck ever will.

In **Chapter 18**, I'm going to walk you through some actual deals we've done—case studies of properties we picked up for $10,000, $40,000, $70,000... and flipped for six figures in net profit. I've also done more 7 figure deals than I can count. This is where the theory turns into reality, and you get to see how the sausage really gets made.

I've told you about the why, I've walked you through the what, and now I want to lay out the **how** with **real-life case studies**. These are deals that came from the exact same process I've been preaching—pulling lists, getting on the phone, being honest with sellers, solving complex problems, and buying property way below market value.

These aren't theories. These are real deals. Real margins. Real numbers.

CHAPTER EIGHTEEN

CASE STUDIES:

REAL DEALS, REAL MONEY, REAL PROBLEMS

Now before I dive into these case studies, I want you to remember something: every one of these deals looked like a nightmare at first. Title issues. Delinquent taxes. Several owners, maybe a squatter. Confusion about who actually owned the place. If it was a clean, easy deal, it wouldn't have been a deal at all—it would've sold on the open market for full retail price. So what I'm about to show you is what happens when you stop running from problems and start running toward them.

These are not cherry-picked wins. These are representative of what this business model produces when done right, and when you're willing to get your hands a little dirty.

Deal #1 — Noth Texas Infill Lot with 7 Owners
Purchase Price: $70,000
Sale Price: $530,000
Profit: $460,000

I'll never forget this deal. It was in Noth TX—a small ½ acre square foot infill lot with a dilapidated house that had a **demo order** from the city. Most people looked at it and ran in the other direction.

Why? Because there were **seven owners** on title, each scattered across different states, and most of them hadn't spoken to each other in years. It also had $20K of delinquent taxes and one owner swore the house was his, and his alone.

Now most investors would see that and say, "Too many moving parts. Too much family drama." But I didn't see seven problems—I saw seven small negotiations. All in silos I contacted each of them directly. Talked to them one-on-one. Gave each of them somewhere between $2,000 and $10,000. Pending their share and position. The total to the owners was $40,000. Another $30,000 went toward cleaning up the taxes and filing curative title.

All in, I was at $70,000—and we flipped it for $530,000.

That's not luck. That's skill. That's structure. That's execution.

Deal #2 — 24,000 Sq Ft Warehouse in South Texas
Purchase Price: $1.7 million
Sale Price: $3.2 million
Profit: $1.5 million

This one came off a **delinquent tax list**, believe it or not. A massive industrial warehouse—24,000 square feet—had fallen into distress because the **tenant stopped paying** and the landlord was overleveraged and undercapitalized. Taxes hadn't been paid. It was sitting dormant.

I negotiated directly with the owner, agreed on $1.7 million, paid off the taxes, got a new tenant lined up under a new lease, and flipped the whole thing at a 50% markup within 13 months. I'd planned to make it a rental for long term income but the flip profit became too great once the title messes was cleaned up. I had to change gears.

Not only did we make $1.5 million, we did it without doing any renovations. **No drywall. No paint. No contractor headaches. Just hauled trash out and cleaned up the site for maybe $25K.** This was strictly a paper deal—clean title, cleaned-up paperwork, and a better financial story.

Deal #3 — The 65-Owner Parcel
Purchase Price: $250,000
Sale Price: $1,250,000
Profit: $1,000,000

This is one of those where you tell people the story and they say, "No way." But I swear on everything, this is a real deal.

Sixty-five different owners. Yes, sixty-five.

This was a big chunk of land in Central Texas that had been tied up for decades. Every time one owner died, the heirs didn't probate. Title got more tangled than a bowl of fishing line. There were family feuds, lawsuits, restraining orders—you name it. Heck, there were 5 contract memorandums filed in the land records csonce one fo the 10% owners kept trying to sell solo with out the rest of the family.

But here's the thing: most of those owners didn't care anymore. They had long since written it off. They just wanted out. Some took $500. Some wanted more. One person demanded $20,000. We paid $100,000 in taxes and $150,000 to owners. That's it. The real kicker? I thought the land was worth $600,000 when I bought it. Once I cleared the title, had it appraised, and put it on the market, we got **$1.25 million.**

That's how valuable execution is in this business.

Average Deal Snapshot

Now I know those deals sound like home runs—and they are. But I want to ground this with a realistic picture of what **the average deal** in our office looks like. Those deals are with lots of experience and capital but I pulled a 100-deal sample from our CRM, and here's what it showed:

- **Average Purchase Price:** $48,000
- **Average Sale Price:** $194,000
- **Average Net Profit:** $125,000

Let that sink in for a second. Yes, they are smaller than the 3 whoppers I shared, but beat the heck out of the average flip house on wholesale.

We're not out here buying million-dollar mansions. We're buying forgotten lots, burned-out houses, old rentals, and abandoned duplexes, and clearing the mess that nobody else wants to touch. And we're doing it for 20, 30, 40 cents on the dollar.

That's the secret sauce. That's the whole model. I saved nothing for later. You get it all.

It's Not About the Property—It's About the Problems

None of these wins happened because I'm the smartest guy in the room or because I had some fancy funding or a big team. They happened because I ran toward the problem.

I got on the phone. I had hard conversations. I listened. I offered fair terms. I kept my word. I solved the problems. That's not rocket science. I couldn't make it into medical school or law school, but this was attainable. And pays much better.

This business doesn't reward people who know the most. It rewards people who are willing to do what most won't.

That's the real unlock.

In the next chapter, we're going to get into something that most people completely overlook—but it's the single most powerful skill you can build in this business: **talking to sellers the right way**. If you can master communication, you will unlock more deals than any list CRM or data tool ever will.

CHAPTER NINETEEN

TALKING TO SELLERS:

THE HIDDEN SKILL THAT MAKES YOU MILLIONS

If I had to strip this business down to just one core skill—the single thing that separates those who make real money from those who stay stuck—I'd tell you this: it's **your ability to talk to sellers.** That's it.

Not your spreadsheets. Not your CRM. Not your fancy marketing system, your designer business cards, or even that fancy suit. It's your mouth. It's how you handle a phone call. How do you explain value? How you listen. How you earn trust. If you can't get someone on the phone and get them to open up, none of this works.

And let me be clear—this is not about being slick or pushing people into signing contracts. I'm not talking about pressure sales or tricking folks into deals. In fact, that's the fastest way to burn your name and destroy your reputation.

This business lives and dies by **the trust. While some may not lone the model, even saying it's aggressive, they sure can't say its dishonest.**

So, let me walk you through how I handle these conversations—because I've had thousands of them. And I'm not a polished speaker. I don't have some Ivy League sales script. I just talk to people like a real human, because that's what they respond to.

Start with the Truth

When I first call someone up, I'm never pretending to be something I'm not. I don't claim to be a contractor. I don't tell them I'm a private lender or some secret buyer from New York. I tell them who I am.

"Hey, my name's Logan. I'm a real estate operator out here in Texas. I don't like to say investor btw, sounds like a dirty word to some. I came across your property through the county records, and I wanted to see if you had any interest in talking about the decades-old title problems that companies like mine solve for a living." That's it. It's disarming. It's clear. And it immediately communicates two things:

1. I'm not a scammer.
2. I'm not hiding my agenda.

You'd be shocked at how far that gets you in this business. Because people are used to being lied to. They're used to being manipulated. The minute they feel like you're being real with them, they open up. They might still be guarded—but they'll listen.

Listen More Than You Talk

Now, once I get them on the line and they're willing to chat, I don't go into pitch mode. I don't tell them what I think the property's worth. I don't tell them I can close fast or with cash or any of the nonsense wholesalers love to throw around in the first two minutes. I just ask questions.

How long have you owned the property?

Have you been using it?

What's the situation with the taxes?

Do you know if there are any other owners?

Have you tried to sell it before?

And then I shut up and listen.

Because what I'm really listening for isn't just data. I'm listening for emotion. I'm listening for the **real** problem behind the property. Because there's always a story. Nobody lets a property sit for 10 years, unpaid, because they're busy. There's always something deeper.

When you find the story, you find the leverage. Not in a manipulative way—but in a way that lets you solve the problem better than anyone else and make a business case of it.

Be Transparent About What You're Doing

When the time comes to talk about numbers, I don't flinch. I won't sugarcoat it. I don't beat around the bush.

I tell them flat-out:

"Look, if this deal works for me, I'm going to make a good amount of money. That's the goal. If I do this right, I might turn a $30,000 profit or more. But if I screw up—if title's worse than I thought or I can't sell it—I might lose money. I've done both. I'm willing to take that chance if we can come to a deal that makes sense for both of us."

You'd be amazed how many sellers actually appreciate that honesty. I tell them: "If you want top dollar, you're probably better off listing the property with a real estate agent, paying for a few attorneys, and cleaning up the title yourself. If you want to sell it as-is, with all the problems, that's where I come in."

Sometimes they say no. And that's okay. Because when they say yes, it's because they trust me. They believe I can solve the problem. They believe I'll do what I say. And that is because I can.

Don't Promise What You Can't Deliver

One of the fastest ways to ruin your credibility in this business is to promise fast closings when you have no idea what the title situation even is. Also, even the least sophisticated person will lose trust in you as soon as you fail to deliver on the first thing.

I never tell someone I'll close in seven days unless I know for a fact that I can. Many times I close in 1-2 days but usually. Instead, I say: "Here's the deal—I want to get you out of this as fast as possible, but we won't know how bad the problems are until title comes back. If it's clean, we can wrap this up quickly. If it's not, it might take a while. But I'll be upfront with you every step of the way."

I'd rather lose a deal than lie. And I've learned over time, that kind of honesty—especially when things get messy—**earns you deals you never would've gotten otherwise. Plus its nice to have a good reputation, you just sleep better at night.**

Remember: These Are People, Not Leads

This is the most important point I can make.

Every name on that list you pull is a human being. They've got problems. They've got baggage. They've got hopes and fears and years of life behind every decision they've made. And the minute you start treating them like a lead on a spreadsheet instead of a person, you've already lost.

I've had sellers cry on the phone with me. I've had old women tell me they've been waiting for someone to come help them for years. I've had men scream at me and then call back the next day and thank me. This isn't about real estate—it's about connection. Emotional Intelligence is a key skill in distressed business.

In the next chapter, I'm going to walk you through the tools I actually use in this business. Not just software, but how I pull data, how I skip trace, how I track down owners, how I organize all this chaos into a process. Because once you get someone on the phone and they say yes, the real work starts—and you better know how to move fast and move smart.

Let me know when you're ready to keep going.

CHAPTER TWENTY

TOOLS OF THE TRADE:

WHAT I ACTUALLY USE TO FIND, TRACK, AND CLOSE DEALS

Look, there are a million shiny objects in this business. Everybody's pitching some new app or CRM or skip tracing service that's supposed to make your life easier and your deals fall from the sky. I'm not going to lie—some of that stuff can help. But I'm not here to give you fluff or pitch products. I'm going to tell you exactly what we use in my office, what I used when I was solo, and what I still believe works best for folks getting started. Because here's the truth: if your deal flow is weak, it's probably not your tech—it's your effort. But once you've got the drive and you're ready to get organized, here's what I actually use.

1. The List: Where It All Starts

It begins with the data. You can't make money in this game without talking to sellers, and you can't talk to sellers if you don't have their information. So where do we get our lists?

Delinquent Tax Lists. Period.

I've said it a thousand times and I'll say it again: if you want to find truly distressed property owners—folks with real problems— they're on the delinquent tax roll. And I'm not just talking about folks who missed a payment last year. I want them to be two to three years behind. That tells me they're not just procrastinating—they've given up.

You can pull this from:

- Your county tax assessor's office (sometimes free, sometimes a few bucks)
- If you want to pay for convenience, lots of data aggregation of
- Occasionally, we'll build scrapers or hire VAs to help automate certain counties and scrape tax lawsuit filings, but that's not the first step, that's when you have experience and some budget.

But don't overthink it. You only need a few dozen good leads to find a deal. One lead list, well-filtered, is better than 10 garbage ones. Look for older owners, long-term ownership, high dollar amounts delinquent, or folks who live out of state. Usually, it takes 30 leads to get a deal if you're calling this type of list. That's far less than the hundreds you must call when using big data, a dialer, and the volume approach like most wholesalers. Not us, were snipers.

2. Skip Tracing: Finding the People Behind the Property

Now that you've got a list of names and properties, you need to get contact info. Most counties won't give you phone numbers. That's where skip tracing comes in.

Here are the tools I use and recommend:

- **TLOxp** – This is my gold standard. It's not the easiest to get access to, but if you can have relations with private investigators. , it's worth it. Data's clean, deep, and goes beyond just a phone number.
- **Skip Genie or Smart Skip** – Good starter tools. Not perfect, but surprisingly useful. And most importantly—affordable.
- **IDI Core or IRBsearch** – A step up from free tools, worth looking into as you scale.

A quick tip: if you're having trouble getting a hold of the actual owner, don't stop. Call their relatives. Call the neighbor. Call anyone who might know them. Use Google. Use Facebook. Use obituaries. You're not a wholesaler anymore—you're a private investigator who happens to do real estate. This is a huge tip that 90% of investors don't get keep looking, longer than the others who quit early on. That's where the win is.

And don't forget: sometimes the neighbor next door has more info than any skip tracing tool ever will.

3. The CRM: Keeping It All Straight

I'll be honest with you—for the first couple of years, I didn't even use a real CRM. I used a notebook and some Google Sheets. It wasn't fancy, but I knew every lead by heart and I followed up like a bloodhound.

But once you start getting more than a few dozen deals in motion, you need organization. In my office now, we use **Salesforce**—but that's overkill for most people. If you're starting out, try:

- Batch leads provide data, but also have a lead magnet platform inside it, used for years.
- **Trello or ClickUp** – Great for visual pipelines.
- **Airtable** – Super flexible, can be customized to your process.
- **Podio** – A lot of real estate folks use it. Integrates well with automation.
- **REsimpli, InvestorFuse, or other REI-focused CRMs** – These are purpose-built and worth looking at once you've got some traction.

But again, don't fall into the trap of thinking a CRM will save your business. You still have to make the calls, send the offers, and follow up relentlessly. Tools help, but hustle wins. The magic happens on the calls.

4. Title Work and Legal Support

Here's where most new folks screw up—they don't realize how crucial a good title company is. This business is built on fixing broken things, and if your escrow officer doesn't know how to fix stuff, you're going to be spinning your wheels.

So here's what I recommend:

- **Find a title company that understands investor deals.** They need to be okay with delayed closings, creative deal structures, quiet title actions, and curative title work.
- **Build a relationship with a local real estate attorney.** You're going to need them when you get into inherited properties, stripping or settling judgments and liens, curative affidavits, and other negotiations, plus lots of legal paperwork that can fix title issues.
- **Eventually, find a good PI (private investigator) or genealogist.** We use retired FBI agents and genealogists to track down heirs, build family trees, and clean up legal messes.

At first, this sounds like overkill. But once you start doing real deals, you'll see why this stuff is gold.

5. Dispo and Closing Tools

We sell most of our properties on the MLS. That's what I recommend. Nothing more, not even a buyers list. Brokers bring qualified buyers who have been vetted and are ready to buy.

So when it comes time to sell, here's what we do:

- **Clean up the property** (trash out, mow the lawn, board the windows)
- **Take good photos** (we hire local photographers or use mobile services)
- **List it with a good realtor** who understands "as-is" properties and pricing for speed

We rarely do anything fancy. We're not remodeling these houses. We're not flipping them. We clean them up just enough to not scare people off—and we let the open market do the rest. It's just a clean presentation. Simple to walk and understand the property. You'd be shocked how many properties sell for full value—or close to it—once they're just visible and accessible. No need to get cute. Keep it simple.

In the next chapter, we're going to talk about **how to structure deals when you have no money.** Because I know what some of y'all are thinking: "Logan, all this sounds great, but I don't have $50,000 to drop on a distressed house."

Don't worry—I've got you covered. I started with nothing too. And I'm going to walk you through exactly how to make money on these deals **without risking a dime of your own.**

Let me know when you're ready to dive into that.

CHAPTER TWENTY ONE

NO MONEY? NO PROBLEM. HOW TO CLOSE DEALS WHEN YOU'RE BROKE AS HELL

If I had a dollar for every time someone told me, "I'd be doing what you're doing if I had the capital," I'd probably have more money than I've made doing these darn deals. And look, I get it. It feels like a rich man's game when you're staring at a property that's $50,000 and you've got $22 in your checking account. But I'm here to tell you right now: being broke isn't a barrier—it's a test. And if you pass that test, you're gonna be in a whole different financial bracket real damn soon.

Because here's the truth: I've made money on dozens of deals where I didn't use a single dollar of my own money. No lie. Not for the purchase. Not for the rehab. Not even for the taxes. And it's not because I had a rich uncle or a line of credit—it's because I understood the most powerful phrase in this business:

"Good deals find money."

Let's break this down.

Step One: Get the Damn Deal First

I don't care if you don't have a penny to your name. That doesn't matter right now. What matters is finding a property that's worth $150,000, and getting it under contract for $50,000. That's where this whole thing starts.

When I was getting rolling, I would tell sellers straight up: "Look, I don't have a check in my pocket today. I don't know how I'm going to ultimately close this but I have a network of investors, and I'm going to bring it to the table and figure it out. But I need a little time."

I did build some cash from my land portfolio, but even that took some time. Honesty wins more than flash. Sellers respect transparency more than bullshit. So stop trying to act like you've got a suitcase full of cash—just get the property under contract with terms that give you some runway.

Step Two: Use Option Contracts and Long Closes

You don't want to go out there tying up deals with hard earnest money and 7-day closes when you haven't even figured out who's funding it yet. That's how you get yourself in trouble.

Instead, use a simple **option contract** or a **purchase contract with a long inspection and close date**. Give yourself 30-45 days. That gives you time to:

- Verify title
- Find a buyer or funding partner

- Solve any lingering problems
- Lock in your exit

Remember—there's no rush if you control the asset. You can always come back to close in a day or two once your ready, but give some space starting out.

Step Three: Partner Up Smart

Now that you've got the deal locked up, here's where the magic happens.

You've got three options:

1. **Take it down yourself**-it's the most common to me, this is how I do 90% of my deals, maybe 95%. It does require capital, but figure it out, this is worth it.
2. **Double close the deal.** You line up your buyer and close both transactions same day or back-to-back. Title companies can help you through this. It's clean, quick, and you get your check without ever bringing money to the table.
3. **JV with a real investor (like me).** This is my favorite option for folks just getting started. Bring me a deal, I'll fund the purchase, cover the title work, handle the problems—and when it sells, we split the profit. You learn, you earn, and you don't risk a dime. This is hard to mess up.

If you go this route, I'll tell you what I tell everyone: I don't need tire-kickers or people sending me 30 junk leads. I want a one good one. Find me someone who owes taxes, owns the house free and clear, wants to sell, and can sign a contract. That's the person I want to talk to. Just make sure they have an idea of what they are looking for in the price discussion and is reasonable. I can take it from there.

Step Four: Let the Title Company Do the Heavy Lifting

People think once they have a contract, they need to hire a team of lawyers, set up entities, and figure out tax structures. Stop overthinking it.

Send that contract to a good title company and take it one step at a time.. They'll run title, find the liens, tell you what needs fixing, and in most cases a decent attorney will, help you fix it. You don't need to know everything—you just need to know how to start. This skill will also develop with time. Today I know what to do, the lawyers just do the work, but I have the strategy.

If title says the deal's clean, great. If it's messy, even better—less competition. Just don't panic when problems show up. That's where your money comes from.

Step Five: Close, Cash Out, and Repeat

Once the title's clear you fund it, your partner funds it, or your end buyer closes, and you walk away with a check. You didn't risk much money. . You didn't swing a hammer. You didn't do a single remodel or deal with a city inspector. You just solved a puzzle that no one else wanted to touch.

And that's the business.

So if you're sitting there telling yourself you can't get started until you save $20,000, I'm telling you flat out: you're wrong. What you need to do is find a deal, build trust with a seller, and reach out to someone who can help you close it. Start with a few grand and let's get going.

We'll go deeper in the next chapter about exactly how to **talk to sellers**, how to **build trust**, and how to **get folks to sign contracts even when they're skeptical, emotional, or straight-up combative**. Because this is where most people stumble. They find a hot lead and then freeze up when it's time to actually have the conversation.

CHAPTER TWENTY TWO

TALKING TO SELLERS: THE ART OF THE CONVERSATION

Now this is the part where the whole thing lives or dies.

All the data in the world, all the software, all the skip tracing tools, none of it matters if you can't pick up the phone, call the seller, and have a real, human conversation. I'm not talking about reading a script like some boiler room clown. I'm talking about actually listening, building rapport, and learning how to uncover the real reason they're stuck.

See, when you're working distressed deals, you're not talking to someone who woke up and said, "I feel like selling my house today." You're talking to someone in pain. Financial pain. Legal pain. Emotional pain. So you better damn well approach it with some humility and patience.

What I always tell people is this: don't try to *sell* them anything. Just talk to them. Ask them questions. Try to understand the situation. Ask how long the taxes have been unpaid. Ask if the house is vacant. Ask how many other family members are involved in the title. Ask if they've tried to sell it before. If you do that long enough and earn their trust, they'll tell you everything—and more often than not, they'll ask *you* what to do next.

When that moment comes, you be honest. Tell them what you think it's worth. Tell them the truth about what problems you see and how much work it'll take to fix them. Then you ask them if they want you to help.

If they do—good. You get a contract signed and start working. If they don't—no harm done. Stay friends, leave the door open, and move on.

Some of my best deals have come from sellers who told me no the first two or three times I called. But because I didn't burn the bridge, they came back around when they were ready. You just never know, so you always leave the door open.

CHAPTER TWENTY THREE

THE EXIT STRATEGY: GET PAID AND GET SMART

Once you've got the property under contract, or you've taken title, it's time to execute the exit.

Now here's the thing a lot of new folks get wrong: they focus too much on what they *could* do and not enough on what's the *smartest and fastest way* to cash out.

You don't need to build a rental portfolio with your first deal. You don't need to flip it or remodel it. You don't need to turn it into a boutique Airbnb. You need to make a profit and move on.

Get it listed. Price it right—meaning a little below market so it sells quickly. Let the realtor bring you a buyer. Collect your check. Yes, you can keep a few of these later, once you've got money stacked and you're not living deal to deal. But in the beginning, you've got to stay focused on turning deals fast. You need momentum. You need liquidity. You need experience.

I don't care how good the numbers are—if holding a property ties up your cash and slows you down, it's hurting your business. Cash is oxygen. When you're growing, you need to breathe.

CHAPTER TWENTY FOUR

BUILDING THE MACHINE

Once you've got a few deals under your belt, you'll start to realize something powerful: this is repeatable.

It's not luck. It's not timing. It's not some once-in-a-lifetime opportunity. It's a system. You find distressed property. You build trust. You solve problems. You buy low. You sell for a profit. Rinse and repeat.

And at some point, you're going to need help. That's when you hire an assistant. Maybe you bring on a caller or someone to help with the research. Maybe you JV with someone who's good at the things you're not.

You start organizing your leads, tracking your follow-ups, and building relationships with title companies, private lenders, and realtors. That's when this becomes a business—not just a hustle. And let me tell you: that's a good feeling.

When you go from chasing a check to running a machine that prints them—that's when the game changes.

CHAPTER TWENTY FIVE

THE LIFE THIS BUSINESS BUILT

When I look back at where this all started—some oil field trailer in the middle of nowhere, with my bank account on fumes and a head full of regrets—I realize this business didn't just change my finances. It changed me.

It taught me how to bet on myself.

It taught me how to fix things that were broken—starting with my own damn life.

I've bought warehouses, I've sold thousands of lots, I've built a team, helped friends, and made money beyond what I ever thought was possible. But what I'm proudest of is the fact that I took a shot. I got back up after screwing it all up. I learned. I got serious. I started over. And it worked.

You can do that too.

This business doesn't care about your past. It doesn't matter how broke you are or how much you've messed up. It only cares about how resourceful you're willing to be. Can you learn? Can you talk to people? Can you spot a problem and figure out how to fix it? If the answer's yes, then I don't care if you've got a dollar to your name—you're in the right place.

So go find that first deal. Make that first call. Take that first leap. Because this business can give you everything—if you're willing to go earn it.

I'll see you out there.

— Logan

Summary Page

What You Just Learned — And What to Do Next

If you made it this far, you're already miles ahead of most people. Here's what we just unpacked:

- You learned what distressed property really is—and why most people avoid it.
- You saw the math behind the model: buy it for 10 to 50 cents on the dollar, clean it up, list it, and get paid.
- You learned where the deals are: on tax delinquent lists, in courthouse records, buried inside title messes, and ownership disputes.
- You learned how to talk to sellers—by being transparent, helpful, and honest.
- You learned that you don't need money to start—just hustle and the right partnership.
- You learned the difference between wholesalers, flippers, and the lean, high-margin model we run here.
- You saw what a real business looks like when it's built on solving the hard problems nobody else wants to deal with.

- And you saw real-life numbers—case studies that show exactly how this model works.

But here's the deal: reading this doesn't change your life. Doing it does.

So print that first tax list. Make the calls. Lock up that first deal. Find your first messy probate, your first lien-infested lot, your first abandoned house. And get to work solving it.

Your first check is going to change everything—not because of the money, but because of what it proves:

That you can do it. That it works. That your life is in your hands now.

So go chase the problems. That's where the good stuff is.

I'll be here if you need me.

-Logan

Distressed Property Glossary

By Logan Fullmer

As-Is Value

What the property is worth today, in the condition it's sitting in—warts, trash, broken windows, liens and all. Not what it *could* be worth. What it is worth *right now*. That's the number I base my entire business model on.

ARV (After Repair Value)

What rookies love to talk about. The theoretical value after all the remodeling, holding time, risk, and delays. In my office, ARV is a dirty word. We don't mess with fantasy numbers. We buy based on as-is value, period.

Title Defect

Any issue in the property's ownership or paperwork that keeps it from being sold cleanly. Could be a lien, an old mortgage that was never released, a missing heir, a broken chain of title. These are the cracks in the foundation where we make our money.

Delinquent Tax

When someone hasn't paid their property taxes and is falling behind. It's usually the first red flag in a sea of distress. The best leads come from these lists—because when they stop paying taxes, they've likely got bigger problems you can help solve.

Option Contract

A real estate contract with a built-in "get out of jail" clause. Gives you the right—not the obligation—to buy a property within a time window. It protects you from eating a bad deal while you figure out the mess.

Equitable Interest

The legal leverage you hold once you've got a signed contract. It means you've got a stake in the game, even before you own the property. That's what allows you to partner, assign, or close with power.

Heirship

When a property is passed down to heirs—usually without a will or probate. This is where 70% of our deals live. It's also where families fight, titles get messy, and opportunities sit untouched for years.

Judgment Lien

When someone owes a debt and the court slaps a lien on their property to secure it. These scare most buyers off. Me? I see it as a coupon. It's another lever to negotiate and drive the price down.

Quiet Title

A legal process used to clear up title defects—especially when ownership is disputed or unclear. You file a suit, get a judge to rule on the real owner, and clean up the mess. It's slow, but sometimes it's the only way to clear the runway.

Sub2 (Subject-To)

When you buy a property "subject to" the existing mortgage staying in place. You don't pay it off, you just take over the payments. It's risky if you don't know what you're doing—but a goldmine if you do.

Skip Tracing

The art of tracking down property owners—especially when they've vanished. You use tools, databases, neighbors, and old-fashioned hustle. Sometimes it's like a private investigation. And that's where the money hides.

Probate

The court process of handling someone's estate after they pass. If you want to make real money in this game, you better get comfortable reading probate filings and talking to heirs. It's where the majority of unsellable, golden opportunity property sits.

Mechanic's Lien

A lien was filed by a contractor who wasn't paid for work on a property. These are common on half-finished remodels or abandoned flips. They clog title but are often cheap to negotiate out.

Redemption Period

The window of time a former owner has to reclaim their foreclosed property by paying off debts. Not every state has this, but you better know if yours does—because it changes your risk if you're buying after the auction.

Equity Spread

The difference between what you bought it for and what it's worth. It's your safety net. It's your profit. It's your margin for error. I don't do deals unless I've got a fat spread—because that's what lets you sleep at night.

Lien Stack

When there's not just one lien on a property—but a whole parade of them. Tax liens, mechanics liens, judgment liens, unpaid utilities. Most investors run from these. I run straight at them.

Chain of Title

The official timeline of who has owned a property and when. If that chain is broken—meaning a deed was never filed, someone died without transferring title, or the paperwork is wrong—you've got a title issue. And possibly a great deal.

Memorandum of Contract

A document you record in county records to show you have a contract on the property. It protects you if someone tries to back-door the deal and cut you out. Use it wisely—and always when the deal's juicy enough.

Curative Work

The process of fixing title defects. That's what we do all day in my shop. We don't just flip houses—we fix problems that keep others from doing the deal in the first place.

Undivided Interest (Real Estate):

A form of ownership in which two or more individuals hold title to a property together, without physically dividing the property among them. Each owner has the right to use and enjoy the entire property, regardless of their individual share. For example, one person may own a 25% undivided interest and another a 75% interest, but neither can claim a specific portion of the land as exclusively theirs.

Foreclosure (Real Estate):

A legal process that allows a lender to recover the balance of a loan when a borrower defaults, typically by selling the property used as collateral. Foreclosure results in the loss of the borrower's ownership rights and is carried out through either judicial or non-judicial means, depending on state law and the terms of the loan.

Judicial Foreclosure:

A type of foreclosure that requires the lender to file a lawsuit in court to obtain a court order to foreclose. The borrower is notified and given an opportunity to respond. If the court rules in favor of the lender, the property is sold at a public auction under the supervision of the court.

Non-Judicial Foreclosure:

A foreclosure process that does not involve the courts. It is permitted only if the mortgage or deed of trust includes a "power of sale" clause. The lender must follow a series of legal steps, such as providing notice to the borrower and posting the sale publicly, before selling the property at auction. This process is generally faster and less expensive than judicial foreclosure.

Code Compliance Municipal Lien (Real Estate):

A legal claim is placed on a property by a city or local government when the property violates local codes or ordinances—such as building, zoning, health, or safety regulations—and the owner fails to correct the issue or pay associated fines. These liens can accrue daily penalties and must typically be paid before the property can be sold or refinanced. Municipal liens take priority over many other claims and can lead to foreclosure if left unresolved.

Mortgage Lien

A voluntary lien is placed by a lender when a borrower takes out a mortgage. It gives the lender the right to foreclose if the borrower defaults.

Tax Lien

An involuntary lien placed by the government for unpaid property taxes. It often takes priority over other liens.

Judgment Lien

A court-ordered lien resulting from a lawsuit, where a creditor can claim a debtor's property to satisfy a monetary judgment.

Mechanic's Lien (or Contractor's Lien)

Filed by contractors, subcontractors, or suppliers who haven't been paid for labor or materials used to improve the property.

HOA or Condo Association Lien

Filed by a homeowners' or condominium association when an owner fails to pay dues, assessments, or fines. These can lead to foreclosure in some states.

IRS Tax Lien (Federal Tax Lien)

Filed by the Internal Revenue Service for unpaid federal income taxes.

Credit Card or Personal Loan Judgment Lien

Arises when a credit card company or lender sues the debtor and obtains a court judgment, which then becomes a lien on the debtor's real property.

Attorney General Lien (Real Estate):

A legal claim is filed by a state's attorney general, typically for unpaid fines, penalties, or restitution resulting from enforcement actions, such as consumer protection violations or fraud. It attaches to the property and must be resolved before the sale or transfer.

Attorney General Lien for Unpaid Child Support:
A lien placed on real estate by the state attorney general's office when a parent owes back child support. It secures the debt and must be paid before the property can be sold, refinanced, or transferred.